Leading
Healthy Groups

A Guide for Small Group Leaders

ALLEN WHITE

Printed in the United States of America

First Printing—August 2018

Cover Photos courtesy of 123rf.com

Author's Photo courtesy of Sam White, swautophotography.weebly.com

Books by Allen White

Exponential Groups: Unleashing Your Church's Potential

All In Study Guide: The King's Witness

Living a Balanced Life: Daily Readings

Becoming a Neighboring Church
with Rick Rusaw, Brian Mavis, and Krista Petty

Back to Church
with Pastor Michael Phillips

CONTENTS

1

Preface

This book contains answers to real questions from real group leaders.

In the two churches I served, New Life Christian Center, Turlock, California and Brookwood Church, Simpsonville, South Carolina, leaders asked questions in meetings, in hallways, by email, and through surveys. What I soon discovered was that most of the answers were meaningful to all of the group leaders. I would either pull them together for a meeting on these topics or stand in front of a whiteboard and answer their questions on the spot. This led to a blog for my leaders where I responded to their questions and shared the answers with everyone.

I expect that some people will read this book from start to finish. Others will use this book as a ready reference when a group situation presents itself or a problem arises. Since some readers might only use a section of the book at a time, in order to give a complete answer, I have repeated some information in various sections that you will find elsewhere in the book. The redundancy is intentional. I would rather that you have all of the information in one place when you need it rather than assuming you've read the rest of the book when you're searching for a quick answer. You will also discover that I'm a big advocate for group agreements.

I may not address every question you have, but this book hits on a bunch of them. Some of the sections come from blog posts. Other sections contain brand new content. If your question is not addressed, then ask your coach or small group pastor.

Welcome to a wonderful adventure. Now that you have stepped forward to lead a group or are currently leading a group, you have made yourself available for God to use you. And, he will! There is no more thrilling experience than to allow God to minister through you to your group members. You will see prayers answered. You will see lives transformed. You will witness potential leaders growing out of your group.

That may sound like a lot, but it's not your work. It's God's work in you and through you. Your role is making yourself available to fulfill God's purposes in your group.

Technically, small group leadership is not difficult. There will be situations in the lives of some of your members that arise as you share life together. But, everyone will be grateful they have the group when they have to face hard things. Your job is not to solve their problems or have all of the answers. You are there with the group to walk alongside others as they face trouble and celebrate accomplishments. When members are down and discouraged, it's the group who prays and brings them back to God.

A big part of making disciples is rubbing off on each other. Making disciples does not require perfect people or else God would have no one to work with! There is more of God in you than you might even realize. The Bible tells us that the same power which raised Jesus from the dead resides in every believer (Romans 8:11). We also know that "greater is he who is in us than he who is in the world" (1 John 4:4). Let God, who resides in you, rub off on others.

If as you open these pages and start leading your group you ever feel inadequate, after over 35 years in ministry I just have to say, Welcome to the Ministry! If you ever feel that you are not enough, remember God is enough. Ask for his help.

May God bless you on this journey,

Allen

Introduction: What is a Healthy Small Group?

I suppose if you're going to lead a healthy small group, it would be a good idea to know what a healthy one looks like. Plenty of examples come to mind of unhealthy groups -- groups where one member dominates the discussion; groups that have great Bible studies, but don't live out what they've learned; groups that become unto themselves and never attempt to reach others; and groups that just hang out, but really don't ever move in any direction. But, our focus is on health, not the opposite.

Healthy groups fully accept every member. Every person matters to God and should matter to your group. Some group members might be a little rough around the edges or challenging to meet with, but none are less important or more important than anyone else. God has a reason for putting them in your group. Groups have to accept people where they are, because they can't accept them anywhere else, can they? Acceptance is communicated through listening and giving equal time. Acceptance is expressed through intentionally getting to know those who are different from you instead of instantly gravitating toward those you are fonder of. Jesus directed groups this way, when he said, "Love one another" (John 13:34) and "By this everyone will know that you are my disciples, if you love one another" (John 13:35). Jesus modeled this in who he associated with: tax collectors like Matthew; sinners like adulterers and bad hand washers; Samaritans who were racially different; and many others who the religious establishment looked down upon. Acceptance is one of the most precious gifts any person can give another. Healthy groups accept others.

Healthy groups center themselves on God's Word, the Bible. One of the key purposes of a healthy group is to become more like Christ. Every group has three powerful resources at their disposal to grow in Christlikeness: the Bible, the Spirit, and the group. Paul writes, "Do not conform to the pattern of this world, but be transformed by the renewing of your mind" (Romans 12:2). This transformation takes place through each person's willingness to surrender, the direction of Scripture, the power of the Spirit, and the support of the group. These ideas will be more thoroughly explained in Chapter 5. Regardless of the type of group you lead, these elements are essential for healthy groups to make disciples.

Healthy groups are serious about helping their members grow (and group members are open to receiving help). This could involve encouragement and support to start a good habit or break a bad one. This can also involve confronting sin in the lives of their members. For most people, encouragement is much more appealing that confrontation. While the group should accept people as they are, the group should also love them enough not to leave them there. As the group grows in their relationship with others and their relationship with God, the group cannot shy away from hard things. Healthy groups are serious about help.

Healthy groups live like Jesus was serious about what he said. When Jesus told his disciples that out of 633 laws in Scripture only two rose above the rest: love God and love others (Matthew 22:37-39), he intended for his followers to love God and love others above all else. Jesus wants his followers today to treat "the least of these – the hungry, the naked, the prisoner, and others who lack basic needs" as if they were serving Jesus himself (Matthew 25:31-46). While taking all of Scripture into account, Jesus wants his disciples to surrender themselves to God and live life in a selfless way. He wants his followers to "go and make disciples," baptize them, and teach them to obey all Jesus commanded (Matthew 28:19-20). What if these weren't just suggestions for better living? What if these weren't merely nice platitudes where you could hit a mental "like" button? What if Jesus was serious about what he said? What if he expects his followers to actually do it? Obeying Jesus is a sign of group health.

Healthy groups are on mission. The group is not just about itself. Groups members should constantly seek out people they and the group can serve. Who is the next person to invite? What neighbor needs help? Where can the group serve together locally or globally? Sometimes the greatest coping strategy for dealing with life's woes is to focus on someone other than you. When groups align their mission with Jesus' mission, they benefit from walking in obedience to Jesus' commands. They benefit those who they serve. But, most of all, they benefit themselves with not only the blessing of obedience, but with a new depth of understanding God's teaching through their experiences.

Healthy groups multiply. This is not a popular topic among small groups in North American culture where groups want to stay together forever. I both understand and respect that desire. It's natural to form a bond and "keep the family together." But, it's supernatural to think of others and the groups they will need. I don't mean to sound spooky, but our connection to God is supernatural. His guidance through prayer and the Bible is supernatural. This makes identifying and developing new leaders possible. This causes hearts to change in favor of every disciple making disciples. To reach the world, and especially the next generation, this sort of selflessness is required. Every group should seek God about its direction and its future.

Your group may find other values in addition to these that you desire to integrate into your group life. You can certainly add these to your Group Agreement (see page 44). But, don't replace any of the priorities mentioned here.

That's a lot to think about. These are things to focus on and strive toward. The accomplishment of all of these things will take a lifetime. But, on the other hand, nothing will ever be accomplished if you don't start today. Today is both the culmination of what your life has become and the first step toward what you life will be. Your group is a big part of that.

CHAPTER 1
STARTING YOUR GROUP

Before you start your group, there are a lot of questions to answer. As you read through this chapter, take time to reflect on what kind of a group you want to start and who you will invite.

What's the Purpose of Your Group?

Your purpose must be clear. Otherwise, you'll never know whether your group was a success. No group can be everything for everyone. You must define what your group is, which also defines what your group is not.

Groups can form in a variety of ways. Bible studies focus primarily on studying God's Word and personally applying it. Serving groups could be a team who serves together at church. This could include ushers, greeters, worship team members, teachers, or any other serving team. A group like this would help to develop relationships among those who regularly serve together. Many people start serving because of a need, but keep serving because of a relationship. The meetings could include a Bible study, testimony, and/or prayer time. But, the reason the group has joined together is for the purpose of serving.

Connection groups can vary based on the degree of commitment by the members. Many churches see connection groups as a means of assimilating new members. While this is certainly one function of small groups, it doesn't have to be the only function. Connection could also mean sharing life together – supporting, encouraging, and celebrating the ups and downs of life. Members can offer a helping hand or an encouraging word. Many of these groups operate with a biblical concept of koinonia meaning "communion or fellowship." This is a deep connection well beyond casual acquaintance.

Disciple making groups operate for the express purpose of fulfilling the Great Commission, "Therefore go and make disciples of all nations, baptizing them in the name of the Father and of the Son and of the Holy Spirit, and teaching them to obey everything I have commanded you" (Matthew 28:18-20). This involves both reaching out to others and sharing one's faith as well as "teaching them to obey." The group would focus on what Jesus commanded, but specifically focus on living out what Jesus commanded. Often this includes each group member taking on an assignment from the lesson at the end of each group meeting, living it out through the week, then reporting their progress back to the group or a portion of the group in the next meeting. Disciple making groups are different from Bible study groups, in that, the focus is on application rather than study. But, to avoid splitting hairs, application can be achieved in either group type.

Recreational or activity groups are formed around a hobby or common interest. The activities could range from sports to crafts to making barbecue. While the activity offers a common affinity and reason for the group to form, these groups should also include prayer, a devotional, and/or a testimony in their meetings. This is different from league sports. Believers playing together should "rub off" on each other. Casual conversations could be about anything, but there should also be a spiritual component to these groups. Otherwise, why couldn't these groups form at the city's community center instead of at the church?

Support groups focus on long-term or short-term specialized needs. Groups could meet for short-term support like divorce recovery, grief recovery, or other help during a time of crisis. On-going support is needed for recovery from life-controlling problems, or longer term support for parents who foster and adopt. The focus of the groups is on the issue that brings folks together. Issues can range from healthy living, overeating, alcoholism, drug abuse, pornography, sexual addiction, eating disorders, chronic health problems, and any other need where someone might need consistent, on-going support.

While your group may touch on several different areas, it should focus on one main thing. For instance, your group might be a disciple making group, which might involve fellowship, social activities, serving, and outreach, in addition to Bible study, but the chief aim of your group is in making disciples. How do you know if your group has succeeded? Ask yourself: are we making disciples? This is not just a change or increase in knowledge, but also a change in attitude and behavior.

What your group is about also says what your group is not about. For instance, if a member of a Bible study group is going through a difficult situation like a marital issue or addiction, the group can certainly be supportive of the member while continuing as a Bible study group. If the member needs additional support, then it would be a good idea for the member to also join a support group that focuses on the specific issue. Any member should be welcome to continue with the Bible study group. The Bible study group, however, cannot morph into a support group. Groups can be supportive, but not become support groups.

What type of group do you want to start?

Who to Invite

With your group's purpose clearly in mind, now it's time to consider who to invite. Who is your group for? There are groups for couples, singles, men, women, multiple generations, or a combination of all of the above. Who do you have a heart to reach? Your group could be more specific by choosing a particular affinity – empty nesters, new moms, people in particular occupations, or others. Pray and decide who to invite to your group. Then, make a list of the names that come to mind. Start by inviting those you know.

Once you've decided who to invite, you also need to consider how many people to invite. Groups can have as few as three members or as many as 30 members. Many groups believe they should have 12 members because Jesus had 12 disciples (Matthew 10:1-4). I'm always careful to remind them that Jesus also had Judas, so maybe they should go with 11 members!

Over the years, I've seen group sizes skew smaller. Many groups today have 6-8 members. But, there are still groups of three as well as very large groups. Your meeting place may determine the size of your group (see below). If you intend on inviting more than eight people to your group, you should definitely plan on recruiting a co-leader. You will find more on co-leaders and sub-grouping on page 60.

Check-In with Your Pastor

Your group's connection to the church is vital. As a member or regular attender of your church, you want to check in with your pastor before you invite anyone to your group. While most people are very well meaning in their desire to start a group, the pastor, who is the shepherd of the flock, needs to know what you intend to do. Imagine if an employee of yours decided to set his own hours to fit his schedule without consulting you. How would you feel? How would that affect the overall culture of your workplace? Or what if your child decided to get a part-time job without consulting you first? Since she is only 11-years-old, you would definitely want to know what she's getting into before it happens (or if it's even legal).

I know that you are a responsible adult. But, no one likes things to happen without their knowledge. At a minimum it's disrespectful. At the extreme, it can undermine a pastor's authority. Nobody wants that.

Every believer has a role in the church body. Your pastor's role is to watch over you, care for you, and help you. Talk to your pastor first. Pastors often have resources that will help you get your group started and will help you as you lead your group.

Often churches will have requirements for small group leaders. While meeting the requirements might delay the start of the group, it is important to do all the church prescribes before you start. There are probably good reasons why the requirements are in place.

Some churches have well established small group ministries. Talk to the small group pastor/director about your desire to start a new group. They have the experience and training to help you as you get your group off the ground.

You never want your pure desire to start a group to be misinterpreted as something that is counter to the church's ministry or as some rogue group that is forming. Communication is the key. Be humble and patient as you seek the blessing from your pastor.

When to Meet (Days & Seasons)

Choose a day of the week that works best for you (at least at the start). Over the years, I've seen group leaders move heaven and earth to change a meeting date for a prospective group member only to have the prospect never show up for a meeting. Choose what works for you.

Choose the time of day in the same way, but be a little flexible. Should your group meet in the morning, afternoon, or evening? Again, decide what works best for you, and then be sensitive to the needs of your members. If you make everything very specific to your liking, you might end up being the group's only member!

In planning your meeting day and time, keep in mind that a typical small group meeting is 90 minutes to two hours long. You want to start late enough, so the members can get there on time, yet you want to end early enough so group members can get back to work or home in time to prepare for the next day, especially on a week night.

Some groups meet seasonally. Other groups meet year-round. As your group gets started, decide what pattern works best for you.

Many groups follow the traditional school year for their regular meetings. They start in the fall, then continue until late spring or early summer when school ends. You will find the Christmas season between U.S. Thanksgiving and New Year's Day is a little trickier for regular meetings. This is a time where the group can suspend or end a study, then re-launch the group meetings after the new year. Groups will often do social things together or serve together during the Christmas season rather than conduct regular meetings.

Some groups meet all year. I led a men's group that met every Wednesday at lunchtime for 52 weeks a year. Unless a major holiday fell on a Wednesday, we would meet. While attendance varied during different times of the year, someone showed up for every meeting, even the meetings that I couldn't attend.

Still other groups will start with a commitment to meet for just one study or one semester. They want to have a trial run as a group. This opportunity to test drive a short-term group will help determine whether you really enjoy leading a group, if the group likes each other, and where the group wants to go in the future. Since it's a short-term commitment, it might be easier to get new members to participate. If for some reason, the group is not quite what you had in mind, it's easier to end the group, because everyone agreed to a short-term group.

Where to Meet

Groups can meet in a variety of places. One of the great things about groups is that they are highly flexible. I've seen groups meet in homes, coffee shops, bookstores, workplaces, and even on a commuter train. If you want your group to meet at your church, this is something you should talk to your pastor about. While meeting at the church might be convenient and familiar to people, it's not as personal as inviting someone into your home.

Your home does not need to be large or fancy. It just needs to be welcoming. While you may need to set up additional chairs in the meeting space, you don't want the group to be cramped or uncomfortable. Tight spaces give the impression that there isn't room for new members.

Many different types of groups meet in public spaces – coffee shops, restaurants, libraries, bookstores, workplaces, or other places. These places are obviously easier than meeting in a home, because there's no clean up before or after the meeting. Be sensitive that your group would not be disturbing other customers. Also, be sensitive to the proprietor, in that, you don't want to hamper other business in the establishment. If you know the business owner, your group could possibly meet outside of regular business hours.

This should go without saying, but if the place of business sells coffee or other refreshments, then the group should make a purchase. If the group is in the space for an extended period of time, then leave a very nice tip to the server or the staff. Your group's time at the table or meeting space could have cost them other business. "Pay your rent," if you will. Your group is an example of Christ in these meeting places. Would there be any sense in studying the Bible at someone's business and then being rude or insensitive to them or other customers?

What to Study

What your group studies has a lot to do with what type of group you plan to lead. If you are leading a support group or a group for a specific affinity, then there may be curriculum available to facilitate the group through particular issues. For instance, a group on money management, could use Financial Peace University or Crown Ministries as their curriculum.

For groups centered around a Bible study, there are many options available. Your church might even be doing a church-wide campaign or alignment series where the group study follows the topic for the sermons from the weekend services. Your group members will hear the sermon, then meet together during the week to discuss the topic and make practical application to their lives. This is a great opportunity to start a group, especially.

Some churches provide a sermon discussion guide on a weekly basis, so the group can further explore and apply the Sunday sermon. Often these guides are provided seasonally or in some cases 52 weeks per year.

Often churches give access to a library of curriculum resources for groups or to a streaming video service. Ask your pastor about these types of resources. Typically with a streaming video service, the group purchases the study guides from the publisher, then watches the video from the streaming service.

You want to choose a curriculum that is of interest to your group, but also is in agreement with the teaching of your church. If someone recommends a study from an author or teacher you are unfamiliar with, check in with your pastor to see if the curriculum would be appropriate. Be aware that there are many studies on personal growth, and even spiritual growth, that might be in conflict with the Bible or with your church's doctrine.

When you have chosen a curriculum, it is always wise to let the pastor or your coach know what your group intends to study. They may have some insights into the curriculum that you were unaware of. They might also know of some prospective members who are looking for a study like yours.

When to End the Group

Everything with a great beginning eventually comes to its natural end. The same is true for groups. Some groups last for six weeks, then they are finished. Other groups last for 30 years. Much of this depends on the desire of the group. But, other factors come into place like members relocating to other cities, finding other interests, or passing away. You can find more information on when to end the group on page 145. But, as you begin your group, keep in mind that no group will last forever.

Build in natural check points to get feedback from the group and gauge their desire to continue. This could be at the end of each study or each semester. More on this in the discussion of Group Agreements on page 40.

Typically a group will last for 18-24 months. Some groups plan to naturally end at those points. Other groups will renew their agreement for another 18 months. As mentioned earlier, some groups meet for a six week trial run, then choose to continue or discontinue after that. There is no right or wrong.

Gathering a Group

Once you've received the green light from your pastor, start making a list of who to invite to your group. The best groups tend to start with the people you already know or the people God sends your way.

First, pray about who you should invite to your group, and then pay attention to who crosses your path. God will answer your prayer. Sometimes God will send people your way who you may have never thought to ask. Pay attention to chance meetings or phone calls "out of the blue." These could be clear invitations of who to invite.

Next, make a list of people you know who might be interest in the group and the topic you are studying. Start with your friends, and then expand your list to neighbors, co-workers, church members, acquaintances, people with common interests, and even parents from your kids' activities. Don't limit your list to just church members.

If you send Christmas cards, who could you invite from that list? Who is on your speed dial? Give them a call and invite them. How about your social media? Who do you personally know that might participate in your group?

Once you've made your list, pray about an opportunity to invite them to your group. Watch how God opens doors.

Don't get discouraged if your first choices for group members aren't available or aren't interested in the group. Keep trying. This happens to everybody.

Years ago, a couple in my church in California decided to leave a group they loved in order to start a group. They made a list of 20 people. When I asked them one Sunday how their new group was coming along, they reported, "Not very well. We think we made a mistake by leaving our old group to start this one. We have invited 20 people so far and all 20 said, 'no.' We don't understand. We clean our house. We shower. Maybe this was a mistake."

I encouraged them to keep inviting. "You had an idea of who should be in your group. Now, let's pray and ask God who he wants to include in your group." They agreed.

About a week later, this couple called me. "Please stop sending people to our group. We have 14 people who want to join the group. We don't have room for any more plus all of their children! So, please stop sending people to our group."

How many people had I sent to their group? Zero. We had prayed, and God sent 14 people to their group. That group went on for 10 years.

Invite the people you know and the people God sends your way. Ask expecting a "yes" from each one, but don't get discouraged if you get a "no." Keep asking and keep praying. God will help you gather your group.

In addition to your invitations, have the first people who join the group make their lists of people they know. Your new members can invite other people just as well as you can. Once your group reaches the capacity you've determine either from the size of your meeting space or from the number of people you think you can keep track of, then stop inviting temporarily. I believe groups should always be open to new members, but when you've maxed out the meeting space, you have to invite more strategically as you move forward.

Over time some of your group members might move away or can no longer attend the group. Some might leave to start their own group. This is normal group behavior. As you and your group continue to invite and include new people in the group, your group can navigate the ups and downs of group life.

What are you waiting for? In the lines below, write down the names of your friends, family, co-workers, neighbors, and others who you might invite to your group. Visit this page daily to pray over these names, and then invite them when you have the opportunity.

_____ _____

_____ _____

_____ _____

_____ _____

_____ _____

CHAPTER 2
STAYING HEALTHY AS A GROUP LEADER

Leading alone doesn't make any sense. Every leader needs relationships outside of the group that will encourage them and help them in leading the group. As a leader, you need to improve your leadership as well as accomplish your own spiritual next steps. This is where a coach will help you.

You Need a Coach

Group leaders never count on the loneliness of leading a group. You would think that connecting to a group of people on a regular basis would cure loneliness. Yet your experience as the group leader is different than the experience of the group members. Now, don't get me wrong. You will participate in the group meetings and activities just like everyone else does. After all, you are a member of the group. But, as the group leader, you do operate from a different viewpoint.

I discovered this on retreats with my group leaders. One of the greatest takeaways from every retreat was the connection and interaction the leaders had with each other.

In fact, the first year we did groups at our church in California, all of the group leaders quit after 12 months, because they felt like lone rangers. They needed someone in their corner to guide them, coach them, and cheer them on. Everyone does.

This is where a coach or mentor comes in. A mentor typically is someone who is spiritually mature, but not perfect, and has experience beyond yours in leading a small group. If you're a new leader, then a coach can give you direction in getting your group started. If you become discouraged in forming your group, your coach can offer support and advice. Most of all, they can offer a listening ear and prayer support for your efforts.

If you've been a group leader for a while, then a coach can help you stay on track with the mission of your group. They will encourage you and keep you going through potential dry seasons of ministry. They've been there. They know.

Your coach is also someone to turn to when you have questions about things that happen in your group or about the curriculum. They might not have all of the answers, but they will have many answers from their experience. When you come up with something they can't answer, then you can either figure it out together or take the question to a pastor or a member of your church's small group team for the answer.

Some churches provide coaches or mentors to their group leaders. If this is the case, then your pastor or small group director will probably introduce you to a coach as you are beginning a group.

If your church does not have a coach for you, then pray about inviting an experienced group leader to coach you. While they are already busy leading their group, chances are they will be honored by your request. The two of you can decide how frequently you want to connect and by what means. Some coaching takes place by phone calls or text messages. Other coaching happens over cups of coffee or quick connections in the lobby at church. Choose a plan of action for two or three months, then evaluate how the relationship is working for both of you.

The biggest part of coaching is developing a relationship with each other. Coaching works best when both are comfortable with each other and begin to understand each other. Due to the potential closeness of a coach and a group leader, it's best to have a coach of the same gender, so their interest and encouragement is not taken as something more personal.

Your Example as a Leader

No small group leader is perfect. In fact, no one is. When it comes to measuring up, most small group leaders fall short just like everybody else. That's the simple truth. You're not the only leader who fought with your spouse right before the doorbell rang and your first group member arrived. You're not the only group leader who's lost your temper, then felt the need to paste on a smile. What do you do when you feel like you don't measure up to God's standard? Should you stop leading? If that's the case, everyone would stop leading.

In the Bible, David asks, "LORD, who may dwell in your sacred tent? Who may live on your holy mountain? The one whose walk is blameless, who does what is righteous, who speaks the truth from their heart" (Psalm 15:1-2). While every believer should all strive to become more like Christ, if perfection is the qualification, then that sounds like a pretty empty sacred tent.

Every person on the face of the earth has fallen short (Romans 3:23). No exceptions. There are no perfect people. Now, this isn't an excuse for bad behavior. It's just the simple truth that even at our best, people just don't measure up. Fortunately, there is also good news.

If the requirements are to be blameless, righteous, and truthful, everyone fails to meet those requirements. But, Jesus is blameless (Hebrews 4:15), righteous (Romans 5:17), and the Truth (John 14:6). Some would say the solution is to act more like Jesus. The only problem is, no one can live up to that standard either.

Jesus always did the right thing. Jesus always had the right thing to say. He always had the right response to the religious leaders' tricky questions. No one tied Jesus up in knots intellectually. No one got his goat emotionally. Nothing broke his connection with God spiritually. Imitating Jesus is not the answer. No one is that good.

What if you stopped trying to live for Christ and allowed Jesus to live his life through you? Jesus said, "I am the vine; you are the branches. If you remain in me and I in you, you will bear much fruit; apart from me you can do nothing" (John 15:5). Jesus doesn't desire for you to try to become like him with our own efforts. Jesus just wants you to get out of his way, so he can do his work.

Your job is not to work hard on being blameless and righteous. Your job is to remain connected to the vine. Sometimes leaders are so busy with the appearance of the fruit, they forget the connection to the root. Disconnection from Christ doesn't produce fruit. It produces death and uselessness (John 15:6).No one wants that.

How do you remain connected with Christ? First, you keep yourself in constant conversation with Jesus. Not out loud in public places to draw attention to yourself. But, to yourself. Rather than mulling things over and over in your head – replaying old tapes that keep you defeated – you need to talk to Jesus about it. "I don't feel too good about this meeting coming up. What should I do? How should I handle this? Please guide me and help me." And, guess what? He does.

When you read the Bible, it's not for the purpose of discovering more things that you're required to live up to but can't. The Bible reveals God's vision for your life. When you read things that might seem impossible to do, take those things to Jesus: "Jesus, if you want me to be kind and compassionate like you said in Ephesians 4:32, you're going to have to do that in me, because I'm not going to get there on my own." As you surrender yourself and give your natural responses to situations over to Jesus, he will guide your words, your actions and your steps.

Here's the best part – the blamelessness, righteousness and truthfulness required to dwell with God is exactly what Jesus gives you. You aren't blameless. You don't become righteous on your own. You walk in the truth by allowing the Truth, Jesus Christ, to live in you.

What part of your life doesn't look like Jesus? Before you start beating yourself up, ask him to create Christlikeness in you. You just might be surprised at how Jesus can change you for good.

Doing ministry without the power of Christ is like trying to fly without an airplane. People lack the ability. Doing God's work in God's way with God's power will reap God's result. You are not alone.

What is Appropriate for the Leader to Share in the Group

Every believer sins. No one is perfect. Whether you're struggling with temptation or just out rightly sinning, how much do you share with your group? After all, while confession is good for the soul, it is often bad for the reputation. Here are some suggestions in navigating this tricky issue:

There is a tension between being holy and being human. Until you signed on as a small group leader, you were just Joe (or Jane) Christian, sitting in the congregation, dealing or not dealing with your stuff, but then you became a leader. All of a sudden the struggles you felt you could share with your friends, no longer seem appropriate in your group. After all, if as the leader, you continue to fail, won't that only give the group license to fail? This is false thinking.

As Christians we often specialize in ranking sins. While transgressions registered on a radar gun may be permissible, sins registered on a breathalyzer are certainly not. There are different ramifications for different transgressions. You cheated on a test in college. That was a long time ago, you were young. You cheated on your taxes. The IRS will bring more serious repercussions. You cheated on your spouse. That's a huge one. It's all cheating, but very different levels.

What you share and how you share it will determine whether your group creates a climate of openness or a façade of pretending. But, how do you know the right timing to open up to your group?

This is where your coach comes in. If you're not sure what to share in your group or at what level of detail, check in with your coach. If the issue is an active struggle in your life, your coach can point you to the right resources. "But, what if my coach judges me or takes my group away?" First of all, no believer has any right to judge any other believer. Your coach is not your judge.

As far as leadership goes, it really depends on what's currently going on in your life. If it's a past sin, then it's in the past. Let God use your experience to help others. If it's a current struggle, then you might need to step out of leadership to focus on the issue for a time. Your well-being as a believer is far more important than group leadership.

Before you choose to disclose your struggle with your group, ask yourself: Where are you in regard to your struggle? Is it behind you? Is it in front of you? Are you in the middle of it? It's one thing to talk about a struggle you've overcome to inspire or challenge others. Everyone needs God's grace to make it one day at a time.

But, if you're currently struggling with a life-controlling problem or a serious relationship issue, it's time to step out of leadership and address the issue directly. While no leader is perfect, some situations are serious enough to fully deal with now before things get worse. When you've achieved a measure of victory, then it could be time to focus on serving others again.

Why would a leader have to step down? When you're in leadership, you're on the enemy's "hit list." When the pressure's on, he will use your struggle to destroy you, your family, and your group. It's important to resolve this foothold in order to avoid a multiplication of consequences in your life, your family's life, and your group's relationships.

When people lead others, they tend to focus on other peoples' needs rather than their own. Good ministry can actually help a leader avoid dealing with his or her own situation. Sometimes folks are even deceived into thinking that because God is using them, the sin or habit must not matter. But, it matters significantly. The enemy is just waiting for an opportune time when your exposure will do the most possible damage.

In recovery ministry, it's often said that "you're only as sick as your secrets." The power of sin is secrecy. Once you share what's going on with you, you expose your secret to the light of Truth. The hold sin has on you is no longer as great. The help you need is now within arm's reach. The Bible says, "Therefore confess your sins to each other and pray for each other so that you may be healed" (James 5:16). Often believers wish to declare, "This is between me and God." That doesn't work. If you could have quit on your own, you would have quit by now.

As Rick Warren says, "Revealing the feeling is the beginning of healing." A conversation with your coach or your group is the place to start on your journey to healing and wholeness. If you're reluctant to confess to your coach, take an Uber. Confess to the driver. Then talk to your coach.

Every believer struggles with something. Don't beat yourself up over struggling. It means the Holy Spirit is working in you. If God's Spirit wasn't in your life, you probably wouldn't be struggling at all. Allow God's Spirit and God's people to encourage and support your road to recovery.

Working through a Personal Issue with Your Coach

Everyone has a spiritual next step, including you. Many of these next steps will be identified and implemented in your group at the end of every meeting. Based on what the group discussed in the lesson, everyone should set a goal for themselves or choose an assignment for the week, then report back to the group the following week about their progress. But, there may be some areas you want to work on apart from the group.

Your coach can offer support and accountability as you face an issue. He or she may also refer you to other resources, groups, or counseling depending on the nature of your issue. The relationship with a coach provides a confidential place to disclose and work out what you're dealing with.

Your coach will never force you to disclose anything that you aren't willing to talk about. Don't ever feel that pressure. But, when you are ready to deal with something you don't feel like you can bring up in your group, your coach is the right person to start with.

Not all next steps seem so grave. Every leader has good things they want to start in addition to any bad things they want to leave behind. This is where support and accountability come into play.

Maybe you want to start a regular quiet time, become more disciplined physically, or take a step in regular financial giving to the church. Your coach is a great resource to you as you get started. Everyone needs someone to report to and someone to celebrate every small win. You are no exception.

What do you want to work on?

Support and Accountability

The only accountability that works is the accountability that you want. Support and accountability starts with the issue you want to work on as a group leader. Your coach, who is an experienced group leader and a mature Christian, can help you.

On the small group leadership side of things, your coach will help you to navigate any situation that might come up in your group. Even if it doesn't seem to be a major problem, it's wise to consult your coach on anything and everything before the issue grows a deep root and requires a backhoe to remove.

A few years ago, we had a group that was struggling for a number of reasons. One of the biggest issues was they were catering to the preferences of one group member. They studied what she wanted to study. They socialized how she wanted to socialize. She wasn't the official leader, but she was certainly influential.

While the group continued to stay together, frustration continued to build. The members didn't voice their frustration. They expressed it in more passive-aggressive ways.

Everything came to a head when the group changed their pattern of socializing. Originally, the group would go out to dinner once a month just to spend time together and hang out, which is a good thing. This is something I would champion. Eventually, this practice devolved into finding the best Happy Hour in town. While churches and faith traditions vary on their views toward alcohol, the offense in this case was they never bothered to ask if anyone in the group had a problem with this practice. This was a problem in more ways than one.

The problem had grown to the point where even the coach couldn't handle it. The coach took this issue to her direct report, the women's director, who in turn brought the issue to me. When I met with the entire group (along with their coach and women's director), I asked them why they hadn't talked over their Happy Hour practice with the rest of the group. Then, I asked the group if anyone took issue with it. As you might imagine, there were some people very uncomfortable with this. Rather than raising the issue and offending the controlling member of their group, they chose to be offended themselves and avoid those outings. It was time to reel this back in and go back to dinner in the restaurant and avoid the bar. But, this wasn't the true problem.

By allowing one member to control what the group was doing, the group thought they were just getting along. The truth is what they were doing was harmful to the group. It took a coaching conversation and the label "harmful" to get the group's attention. In our conversation with the entire group, the offending member backed down on her demands. I think she acquiesced that "no one else seemed to have any good ideas, so she always offered hers." She didn't consider how she was bullying the group. The group continued after that with more give and take.

The issue for the group never needed to reach this point. If the leader had checked in with the coach (or vice versa), and the leader asked if a monthly Happy Hour would be a good idea, the coach would have given them direction on how to navigate this. Particularly, the coach would navigate them away from Happy Hour. When the issue of the controlling member would have been mentioned, the coach certainly would have cautioned the leader about following this pattern. A sincere conversation with the offending member most likely would have resolved the situation. This woman was not a monster. She could be reasonable. If the leader struggled with the conversation, then they could meet with the coach, but meeting one on one is always the best place to start, even though it might seem like a difficult conversation.

Small issues do not need to become extreme. Don't ever feel like you are bothering your coach by raising an issue. No issue is too small. But, left unattended, small issues can become major problems. Speak to your coach often.

Every leader needs someone who is a little further down the path of spiritual maturity to help and support them. Don't neglect your conversations with your coach. He or she will be honored that you desire their help.

You will find more information on accountability and spiritual growth in Chapter 5: Making Disciples.

On-going Training When You Need It

Training is important to your growth as a leader. The more you grow, the more effective your group will become.

Your main source of training will come from your church and your coach. Every church offers training a little differently. Some churches will hold monthly meetings with small group leaders. Take advantage of these. Some small group pastors will send out blog posts or videos to offer nuggets of training. Your church might offer an annual leaders' retreat, a leadership conference, or even online training.

As mentioned before, your coach is a great training resource because a coach can give you answers right when you need them in the middle of a situation or issue. The training that sticks best is the training you receive when you need it. This is why it's important to reach out to your coach on a regular basis and talk about what's happening in your group – both good and bad.

Pay attention to what's going on in the group ministries of other churches in your region. Maybe another church is bringing in a speaker or sponsoring a training event for their leaders. Check into the possibility of attending their event, or check with your pastor about partnering with the other church for the training. No sense in reinventing the wheel.

Blogs and podcasts can offer valuable training for group leaders. While some may cater more toward small group pastors and directors, you can still benefit from the content. I recommend sources like smallgroupnetwork.com and their Group Talk podcast, smallgroups.com from Christianity Today, The Navigators, smallgroupleadership.com, and of course, allenwhite.org.

Some churches subscribe to curriculum streaming services that also offer leader training from nationally-known teachers. Services like RightNow Media, Lifeway's smallgroup.com, Zondervan's studygateway.com and others are great platforms to receive training.

There are many books about leading small groups. Check out the recommended resource list on page 152. Maybe suggest a book to your coach that you and other group leaders could study together. This creates both a training environment as well as a chance to build strong relationships with other leaders.

One of the best ways to develop yourself as a leader is to train a new leader. Now, you might me saying, "Well, I'm just getting started. I'm not sure how helpful I would be." Here's the deal: whether you've lead for one study or one semester, you have more experience than the new leader who is starting their first group. By sharing what you know in answering their questions, you will also improve your leadership. Check with your coach or your pastor about opportunities to coach others. Some churches might be willing to let you start right away. Other churches might have other expectations or requirements for you to fulfill before they would release you to coach another person. Be available and be patient.

Whether your church provides leader training or you go the self study route, invest in yourself and your leadership ability. What you put into growing your leadership will reap dividends in the lives of your group members.

Avoiding Burnout as a Group Leader

Leading a small group is not meant to burn you out. In fact, it shouldn't. There are ways to avoid burnout as a leader. Let's start with some biblical examples.

Moses worked very long, hard days mediating the disputes of God's people (Exodus 18), and then Moses got some feedback from his father-in-law, Jethro: "What you are doing is not good" (Exodus 18:17).

Moses insisted that he was the only one who could serve the people and that the people liked coming to him. Basically, Moses was co-dependent on the people of God. It made him feel good. But, one detail from this account shows why it wasn't good: Moses' wife, Zipporah and his sons were living with Jethro. Moses' busyness for God had separated him from his family. This was not good.

Elijah called down fire from heaven (1 Kings 18), and then Elijah wanted to die. He started by doing exactly what God had directed him to do. With God's power and direction, Elijah defeated the prophets of Baal. The result was not a big celebration. The outcome was a manhunt, and Elijah was that man. Jezebel wanted his head (1 Kings 19:2). You would think that doing God's work would be rewarded in better ways. Elijah survived for another day, but he was exhausted, depressed and ready to cash it in.

You can avoid burnout in ministry. But, you need to start before the fuse has burned to the end.

First, you don't need to do everything for the group. Pass around the leadership and allow different group members to take on different tasks each week. As the group leader, you can give away responsibility on practically every aspect of your group: leading discussions, hosting the group in a home, bringing refreshments, taking prayer requests, following up on new members and absentees, planning social events, pursuing outreach opportunities, recruiting new members, and other things that come up.

The only thing that a leader can't give away is the overall responsibility for the group. It's up to you to make sure that things get done, but not to do everything yourself. It might be easier to do it yourself. You might like doing it yourself. But look at what happened to Moses. Don't follow that example.

Next, think about balancing the other parts of your life. What else are you doing right now? Most people need to work a job and/or work at home. Maybe you're raising your kids. Some homeschool their kids. Then, there are kids' sports and activities (and boy, that can quickly take over your life).

Beyond activity, you need to consider what changes have taken place recently. What is new this year: a job, a home, a baby, reduced income, cub scouts, or a major health issue? You can only tolerate so much change at a time. Fortunately, God made time so that everything wouldn't have to happen all at once. There are many things you have absolutely no control over. But, if you are feeling the stress of change, then opt out of optional changes for now. That doesn't mean putting off taking that class or losing weight or buying a new car forever, but put it off for now. Maybe wait a year. Count the cost before starting anything new or adding something to an already full schedule.

A co-leader is a big help to avoid burnout. Who really cares about your small group? Who's there every week and calls when they can't make it? Who has shown the ability to lead? Recruit someone to help you. Let them help you.

A co-leader can bring some welcomed relief when life gets to be too much. Everyone needs to take a break once in a while. That doesn't necessarily mean that you quit attending your group, but maybe you go through a season when you let your co-leader take the lead.

The key here is communication. Make sure that you are on the same page with the direction and focus of the group. That's not to say that your way is the only way, but people joined your group for a certain reason. If your group's purpose radically changes, then your group might not tolerate it. Shared leadership requires shared vision.

Sometimes as the leader, you need to take a break from the group. If you find yourself at your wit's end, you need to take a break. If you are burned out, tired, frustrated, or experience health problems, start by focusing on your physical wellbeing. Get enough sleep. Eat right. Get a little exercise. Stepping out of your group will allow you two more hours in the week to do these things. If you don't feel well physically, you won't feel well emotionally or spiritually either.

Once you feel a little more rested, focus on your emotional health. How's your attitude? Do you find yourself scowling or laughing? Are you hopeful or hopeless? On a scale of 1 to 10, where is your cynicism these days? If you're about a six, then you need to recover! Find a way to do some things for yourself. Take a walk. Watch a movie. Invest in your relationships. Hours of television will only slow your recovery. Honest conversations will revive your soul.

Now, this might seem completely backward, but your spiritual health comes last. I used to think: "Lord, I'm doing your work. I'm tired. I'm burned out. I'm frustrated. Give me supernatural strength to rise above the situation that I've created for myself by too many late nights, poor nutrition, and taking on too much. It's all for you God. Help me, so that I can help you."

God's response was usually something like: "Oh, give me a break." God won't bail you (or me) out and reinforce your bad behavior. Constantly violating God's design is a sure path to burnout.

God designed you to work hard. God designed you to rest. God designed you for relationship with him and with others. God designed you for a purpose. God designed you to be fragile. Lives are best lived with an ebb and flow. When you apply effort and energy, then you need to take a break and rest.

The spiritual component is very important because as a group leader, you are a spiritual leader. That doesn't mean you have to be better than your group members. It does mean, however, that you must maintain the vital connection with God for him to work through you in the group.

A daily quiet time should be a regular practice. Whether you have extended time each morning or find yourself on the run, even a few verses of Scripture and a few minutes in prayer is better than nothing. Find time during the course of your day...during your morning or evening commute to work, stepping out the front door for a few minutes and just standing on the porch, waiting for an appointment...and connect with God. Most people don't believe they have time. Just replace the time you spend looking at your smartphone with reading a little Scripture and praying. If you're already looking down at your phone, you're in a suitable position for prayer, right? Head bowed.

Your ministry to the group is not totally up to you. Ministry is God's work through you to the group members. As you maintain the vital connection with God, he can do his work. God's work done God's way won't burn you out.

The reason that you feel physically tired and emotionally negative after a group meeting is that your body, your whole system, is telling you that it's time to get out of group leader mode and relax. It's not a time to evaluate your performance as a group leader. It's not a time to consider quitting the group or moving to Tahiti. It's time to rest. Leave behind the mess that you can tolerate. If another member is hosting, then you can just go home and not worry about cleaning up.

Some ministry leaders take the position that, "I'd rather burnout than rust out." Neither is a very good option. It's much better for you to wear out gradually.

CHAPTER 3
PLANNING YOUR FIRST MEETING

As a new group leader, there are a few things to think about as you go into your first meeting. In fact, there may be too many things to think about. Focus on the basics and you will have a great first meeting.

Prepare.

As the leader of this group, you don't have to be the expert. If you're using video-based curriculum, the expert is the pastor or teacher on the video. Let the video teaching lead the way. Otherwise, just follow along with the instructions in your study guide. But, before the meeting it's a good idea to review the video and the discussion questions.

If you find your group doesn't have time to complete the entire discussion guide, that's okay. Prioritize the questions for the time you have available. As you get to know the group, choose questions that are appropriate for the group. If your group members are well beyond the basics, then maybe skip the easy ice breaker question, and ask more of an application or accountability question regarding their progress in living out God's Word. Budget time for the group to introduce themselves, whether the group is new or is an established group that's adding new members.

Pray for Your Group.

Feeling anxious about leading the group or even feeling inadequate is perfectly normal, especially if you are leading for the first time. The Bible says, "Do not be anxious about anything, but in every situation, by prayer and petition, with thanksgiving, present your requests to God. And the peace of God, which transcends all understanding, will guard your hearts and your minds in Christ Jesus" (Philippians 4:6-7). So how often should you pray? Pray every time you feel anxious. God will give you peace.

When it comes to group meetings, the leader often works hard to make sure all of the details are taken care of. The lesson is studied. The house is cleaned. The refreshments are made or bought. The chairs are arranged. There's a lot of work that goes into a group meeting. But, even though we've worked hard to pull the details together, are we really prepared?

No one knows what exactly will happen at the next group meeting. You don't know who will show up. You don't know what condition they will be in. You don't know who will miss the meeting. But, God knows exactly what's going to happen. Aligning your purposes to God's purposes through prayer is the key to a successful group meeting.

When you pray, you become more sensitive to God's Spirit. As you pray about the meeting, invite God's presence into our group. The group meeting is for God to orchestrate rather than for you to merely follow an agenda. You will become better attuned to the Spirit's leading during the meeting. When should you linger on a point? When should you move on? God will guide you.

Prayer will also help you become more sensitive to your group members. There will be times when a group member chooses to disclose something right then and there, even when it wasn't asked for. What do you do? Start by whispering a quick prayer: "God, should I go with this or move on?" He will guide you.

Sometimes when your members need to share, it doesn't matter what the question or the topic was. It's your job to be there for them. If this turns into a weekly event, then that is another matter. But, an occasional deviation from the schedule never killed any group. As you give the group member freedom and permission, you give them a priceless gift. They don't need have their problem solved. They don't need advice. They just need to be heard. By preparing through prayer, your heart is in the right place to give them this gift.

When you prepare with prayer, you become less disappointed with the result. If you've worked hard to prepare your house and your lesson for the group meeting, then you might be disappointed if just a few, or even nobody, shows up. Why would you continue to work this hard, if no one appreciates it? But, in group life as in the rest of life, the outcomes are up to God.

If only two people come to a group meeting, rather than being disappointed by poor attendance, see it as what God intended for that meeting. What does God want to do with just two people that might not have happened with the whole group there?

As you prepare for your next group meeting pray for each group member individually. Pray for prospective members who have been invited. Pray for prospective members who haven't been invited yet. Pray for God's leading, and then let him lead.

Arranging the Room

The furniture should be arranged so that everyone can see each other during the meeting. This will help in both giving proper attention to group members as they speak and also avoiding the awkwardness of two people starting to speak at the same time. Seeing each other will create warmness in the group.

If your group is meeting in a public place like a bookstore or coffee shop, someone should arrive early to claim the space. Some businesses have meeting rooms or can reserve seating for the group. Make sure you have adequate seating for the group.

If your group is meeting in a home, then you need to have a space where your members can sit in a circle for discussion. If the group is using a video-based curriculum, then the seats should be arranged initially so the group can view the video. Once the video is over, then circle the chairs around for discussion.

If the group wants to meet outside, be sensitive to the surroundings. If the meeting place has a lot of property, then meeting outside should be fine. If the home is in a neighborhood, then meeting outside could create an awkward environment where neighbors could overhear the group conversation. This will certainly cut down on open sharing.

You want to make sure there are more than enough seats for everyone who plans to attend. If you know the exact number of members who will be there, then plan for enough seats plus a couple of extra seats in case a member brings someone new. Again, the seats should be arranged so that everyone can see each other. Often if three people sit on a couch, the people on either end can't see each other. Count the couch as two seats instead of three to avoid this dilemma.

If you are uncertain about how many people are coming, then arrange seating for about half of the group. As additional group members arrive, then add chairs from another room or set up folding chairs. A few padded folding chairs are a good investment for the group.

Your meeting place does not have to be perfect. It's okay if a few things in your home are left undone. It shows that you are just as normal as everybody else. But, on the other hand, you want to make sure that eating areas and the restroom is clean, so no one is uncomfortable with that.

Childcare

Childcare during the group meeting is one of the most important factors in the success of your group. The easier you make the childcare, the easier it will be for your group members to participate. One or a combination of the following methods will help you handle childcare successfully during your group meeting.

1. Recruit someone to do children's ministry while your group is meeting. This could be led by an adult or a teenager in your home during the group meeting. The curriculum could be as simple as a Bible story book, videos of Bible stories, or a church-style children's curriculum from a local bookstore or online.

On the positive side, the children in your group can grow spiritually while their parents are doing the same down the hall. Some groups may have diverse ages of children. The older ones could serve as assistants to the younger ones during the meeting.

The challenge, however, to this method is finding the right person to teach the children during your meeting. You might seek a recommendation from other group members, your friends at church, or possibly a staff member. When approaching a staff member with this request, don't imply that you are giving them the assignment. They have plenty to do already. But, the staff person might be able to recommend someone who is up and coming in chidren's ministry and needs a place to serve.

2. Hire a babysitter. This could be someone you or another group member knows or even a teenager whose parents attend your group. When you invite someone to serve in this way, help them to understand that this is a real job that they will be paid for.

Ask each member of the group to pitch in to cover the cost of the babysitter. NOTE: Be generous to your sitter. You want them back. If you don't pay much, word will spread! Decide on an appropriate amount for each family to contribute for the babysitter. Keep in mind the going rate for babysitters in your area. Once you've decided what the weekly amount from each family should be, add this information to your group agreement (see page 40).

If someone in your group is unable to afford the childcare, then discretely ask other members of the group to cover the cost. Don't allow childcare to become an obstacle to anyone who wants to participate in your group.

3. Allow older children to supervise younger children with adults checking in. This is a different version of the second childcare option. Since there is not an expectation that the older children will provide paid childcare, you can expect to get what you pay for! This method works best with a smaller number of children in the group. Adults would need to check in during the course of the meeting to make sure everyone is okay. Again, hiring a babysitter is a better option, but this method might work in some cases.

4. Ask group members to trade off watching the children during the meeting. Now, this does mean that members will occasionally miss out on a group meeting, or even possibly not show up when it's their turn for childcare, but it is an affordable option for the entire group – no one has to pay! This is a great opportunity for two group members of the same gender to get to know each other better – guys included.

As part of sharing ownership of the group, this could become another responsibility for group members to share along with bringing refreshments, hosting the group in their home, and leading the discussion. This method might be worth a try, then evaluate at the end of the study or semester to see if the group wishes to continue in this manner.

5. Have the children meet in a nearby home. One group in our California church had two families who lived in the same

neighborhood. The children met at the leaders' house with babysitters. The adults met next door at a group member's house. This provided enough distance, so the adults weren't distracted by the children during the meeting. If a parent was needed, however, the adults weren't far away. You might even invite neighbors to your group with this purpose in mind.

6. Allow the children to take part in the group. When this idea is offered up, the typical reaction is "Won't the adults feel uncomfortable to talk about certain things if the children are present?" Here's the deal – groups don't talk about everything. Some people won't share certain things about themselves in front of another's spouse. Those issues are usually discussed outside of the group meeting with the leader or another member anyway.

Another version of including the children is having the children present at the start of the meeting when everyone is gathering, then at the end of the meeting when the group is having refreshments. Someone will need to watch the children during the group discussion, but everyone, including the babysitter, can be part of the meeting. This offers a sense of "extended family" to the group members and their children.

7. Have each member arrange for their own childcare. They may have a regular babysitter, a family member, or someone else who can stay with their children during the group meeting. People find babysitters for all sorts of other reasons, so if they are committed to the group, then this shouldn't be a big issue.

Remember, however, what I said at the beginning of this section: The easier you make the childcare, the easier it will be for your group members to participate. Well, the opposite is also true – the harder you make the childcare, the harder it will be for your group members to participate. If you are starting a new group, then you will want to offer childcare at the meeting place or nearby using one of the other methods listed here.

Years ago, I had a group who ended up with 25 adults and 25 children in their home. The leaders called in a panic. Their group night was pure chaos. Since the group was established, I advised them to have everyone provide their own childcare. This reduced the chaos in their home, and it thinned out the group a little bit. Those who needed on-site childcare found a different group.

8. Trade off childcare with another group that meets on a different night. This is pretty easy. Your group meets on Tuesday and someone else's group meets on Thursday. The other group watches your group's children on Tuesdays, and you return the favor on Thursdays.

Don't stress over childcare. The Bible tells us that God will meet all of our needs according to His riches in Christ Jesus (Philippians 4:19). Pray that God will provide the right childcare solution for your group. He won't let you down! Also, consider asking a member of the group to take the responsibility for arranging for childcare. The member needs to feel needed, and you can move this off of your plate.

The Group Agreement

Every person in a group has different expectations for the group, whether they realize it or not. Some folks have been in groups before and long for the good old days of comfortable koinonia. Others were over-sold on groups: "You'll make your new best friend." Everyone has expectations for the group. The key to successful group life is a thoroughly-discussed and well-articulated group agreement.

The key word is "agreement." An effective group agreement has input from the whole group, and a decision for the group "ground rules" is made together. You are not asking your members to sign a contract that you put together for them. If you impose an agreement on them, you may get compliance, but you won't necessarily get buy-in from the group. People struggle in honoring an agreement they didn't help to create.

Forming a group agreement doesn't need to be a lengthy or hectic process. In a relaxed atmosphere, just get everybody's ideas on the table. Decide on the group's values together. What's important to the members? When and where will the group meet? How will the group provide childcare, if they do? What will the group study? How will the studies be chosen? How will the group spend their time together?

While there are a number of great templates out there, the group agreement needs to fit the group. Imposing someone else's agreement just doesn't cut it. Examples can be helpful, but you're not looking for a good document, you're aiming for a great group.

A group agreement puts all of the members on a level playing field. Everyone knows what to expect. They know what's acceptable and what's out of bounds. From basic, but important, items like when the meeting with start and end, the group will know what to count on. If members need to get back to work after a lunchtime group or put kids to bed on a school night, they will know when it's acceptable to leave.

More importantly, the group agreement insures things like confidentiality. What's said in the group stays in the group. Broken confidences and gossip are group killers. If the group has a party, what will they be drinking or not drinking? If your group doesn't know if any of its members are in recovery, that's an important conversation to have.

How will the group meeting run? While the meeting doesn't have to be the same every week, the members do need to know what to expect. One group I started met in a restaurant for lunch. If we ordered from a menu, then we ordered first, discussed the lesson, ate when the food came, and then pray together. If it was more of a "fast food" place, then we would eat first and ask questions later. While these seem like rather specific details, the reality was that the group members knew what to expect, and the new members quickly understood what was going on.

With a group agreement, everyone knows what is expected of them. Some people are reluctant to join groups because they fear being asked to do something they just aren't comfortable doing. Will they have to pray aloud? Will they have to read aloud? What if they don't read very well? The group agreement helps them understand if these things are voluntary or mandatory.

If members have to miss the group, what is their responsibility to the group? Should they call out of courtesy and let the leader know they will be absent or not worry about it? If it's important that the member informs the group, then put that in your agreement.

As the leader, you shouldn't do everything for your group. It's just not healthy, and it robs others of opportunities to serve in ministry. If your group intends to pass around the responsibilities for leading the discussion, hosting the group, bringing refreshments, leading worship, following up on prayer requests, and whatever else you can give away, your agreement should include the expectation that every member would serve in some way.

Again, what are the values of your group? What is expected of each member? Decide together and from the start of the group inform everyone in the agreement.

Your group agreement will not stand the test of time. Circumstances change. Groups change. While you probably should always include things like confidentiality and shared responsibility, other things like your meeting day, place, time, study, and so forth will change over time. Group agreements should be reviewed at least once per year to make sure that it's still working for everybody.

Group agreements help when new members join. It's important to review key items in your group agreement when new members join your group. You don't have to recite the entire agreement, but important things like confidentiality, childcare details, and so on should be shared with new members. This doesn't have to be formal. You could even say something like "Just to let you know, our group is like Las Vegas. Whatever is said here stays here" or "We're going to order our food, then get into our discussion. When the food arrives, expect a little silence, and then we'll close with prayer."

Your group agreement doesn't need to be overly formal. While it's good to have your group agreement written down somewhere, you don't need to have it notarized or have your attorney present. I have seen some groups simply give their agreement a simple thumbs up. I've seen others sign it like the Declaration of Independence. Do whatever works for your group. Some folks are resistant to words like "covenant," so "group agreement" or "ground rules" would work better for most.

Your group agreement should be the house rules for your group. The rules may change over time, but the most important thing is that the rules work for the whole group right now.

Sample Group Agreement

The purpose of our group is to make disciples through Bible study, accountability, and support.

Our group will meet weekly starting Tuesday, September 9 from 7pm to 9pm to study *All In* by Allen White. If a member cannot attend a group meeting, the member should call the group leader prior to the meeting day and time to let the leader know.

Our group values:

Confidentiality – What is said in the group, stays in the group. There is no place for gossip.

Respect – As a group, we will respect each others' contributions to the group discussion. We will not cut others off while they are talking or talk over people. We will keep the discussion centered on what is directly affecting the group members and not discuss anyone or anything going on outside of the group. We will avoid fixing others and giving advice. We will support and pray for each member.

Genuine Growth – Each week every group member will take

on an assignment, then report their progress back to the group.

Sharing Responsibilities – This is group is not just the leaders' group, this is our group. We will participate by taking turns leading the discussion, hosting the group in our homes, bringing refreshments, planning events for the group, and other responsibilities that come along.

Childcare – The group will hire a babysitter with each family contributing $10 per meeting to cover the childcare expense.

Serving – Our group will find ways to serve others in the community. As needs arise, together the group will help to meet the need.

What If I Don't Know All of the Answers?

For a new small group leader, this question ranks right up there with public speaking and an IRS audit. No one likes to get caught off guard. Fear kicks in. What if you as the leader lose credibility? What if the group doesn't trust you? What if they don't come back? Here's some help in easily navigating this situation in your group.

As the group leader, you are more of a facilitator and not a Bible teacher. If you were teaching a class, then you would be expected to know the answers. Group life is not a top down exercise. Group leaders are not the hub in the center of the wagon wheel. Your Bible knowledge or lack thereof should not jeopardize the group.

Group life is more like a web of relationships. As group leader, you took the initiative to gather the group. You are responsible for the group, but it's not your responsibility to do everything for the group. As a facilitator, rather than a teacher, your job is to get the discussion started and keep it going. You are not the Bible expert. If your group is using a video-based curriculum, the expert is on the video clip. Your role is to ask the questions and help your group apply it to their lives. Your job is not to have all of the answers.

As leader, you are not the sole person responsible for the spiritual welfare of the group. The group is responsible for each other. While that includes you, care is not limited to you.

When someone asks a question that you're not prepared to answer, ask: "What do the rest of you think?" Now, you've bought a little time. Let the group talk. In the process, you might send up a quick prayer, and who knows, you might end up with a solid answer.

When in doubt, the best answer is simply "I don't know." You gain credibility when you're honest, but you definitely will lose it if you try to fake it. No one has all of the answers.Every pastor and Bible teacher gets stumped once in a while. Just confess that you don't know, do a little research, and talk about it again at the next meeting.

You can even go one better than researching the answer yourself. Ask the person with the question to research it and get back to the group. But, a word of caution – not everything on the internet is true. Verify what you've discovered.

Here are some reputable resources that can help:

Christian Research Institute: equip.org

John Piper: desiringgod.org

Apologetics.com

When Skeptics Ask: A Handbook on Christian Evidence by Norman L. Geisler (Baker Books, 1990).

Hard Sayings of the Bible by Walter C. Kaiser Jr (IVP Academic, 2010).

The Case for Christ: A Journalist's Personal Investigation of the Evidence for Jesus by Lee Strobel (Zondervan, 2016).

Of course, one of your best resources is your coach. Whether it's a question you don't have an answer to or a situation that springs up in your group, your coach is an excellent resource to turn to. If your coach doesn't have the answer, then it's time to take the question to the small group team at your church or a pastor.

Remember, the things you and your group learn yourselves will be lessons that last longer. Before you pick up the phone, do a little study for yourself.

Getting Your Group Members to Open Up

Most leaders realize group life extends beyond well-prepared and executed group meetings. While Bible study is an important aspect of a group, if everyone leaves thinking, "Boy, that was good. See you next week" without sharing what's going on in their lives, something is definitely missing. Here's how to help your group open up:

First, set the right expectations. When your group members joined the group, what were they expecting? Were they looking for a 60 minute inductive Bible study followed by brownies and coffee as thanks for surviving it? Were they looking for a free-flowing discussion of everything that popped into their heads? Did they know what to expect?

Managing expectations is crucial for a successful group. Rather than dictate what the group will be or won't be, it's best to start by discussing what kind of group the members actually want. A simple exercise like having everyone write their top three group expectations on a card, then tabulating the results will go a long way in getting buy-in from the group.

If the group skews toward Bible study, then gradually implement some aspects of care. Start with something simple like asking for prayer requests and closing the meeting with prayer. As the group continues to meet, begin to focus more on application questions rather than Bible exploration questions. Don't get me wrong. The discussion should be based on God's Word. But, you want to aim for where the rubber meets the road, not where the rubber meets the air.

Next, set the example. "Speed of the leader, speed of the team" is a common axiom from Willow Creek Community Church. The leader sets the pace. If you are open with your life, then others will be open with theirs. If you hold back, so will they.

A couple of years ago someone gave me an older car. It wasn't perfect, but it was transportation and a gift at that. One night I became frustrated with the dashboard lights. About a third of the lights wouldn't work. Out of my arsenal of mechanical expertise, I pounded my fist of the dash. The change was both immediate and dramatic – I now had no dashboard lights.

Driving in the summer or during the day wasn't a problem. But, anytime I had to drive early in the morning or at night, I had absolutely no idea how fast I was driving. I was embarrassed by my "repair." While I confessed the problem to my wife, I never mentioned it to anyone else.

But, one day a circle of folks in the office were discussing their cars' various ailments. I chose that moment in the safe circle of used car owners to confess my dashboard issue. A woman turned to me and said, "My husband has the same problem with his car. He uses his GPS to check his speed." What a brilliant idea. I had a GPS. I no longer needed to fly blind at night.

I had dreaded the conversation with a police officer who might ever pull me over. "Sir, do you know how fast you were going?"

"No, officer. My dashboard lights aren't working." Somehow I imagined only a scenario with multiple traffic tickets involved. Now, I had the knowledge to detect my own speed and avoid a traffic violation.

I never would have learned that workaround if I had never admitted my problem. Sharing openly has to start with the leader.

I shared this story when I spoke at a church once. The next week, the Executive Pastor called to say that my message already was making an impact. After hearing my story, the man confessed to his men's group that his marriage was on the brink of divorce. He and his wife were separated, and he didn't know what to do. Rather than judge this guy for his situation, his group members rallied around him to support him and his wife through their struggle. My illustration of automotive failure helped him open up about his marital failure.

Group leaders are no better than the group members they lead. You must be careful that the leader title doesn't block the way for your own vulnerability. If you're group isn't opening up, you need to check your own transparency in the group. Your honesty will encourage theirs.

As you set the meeting agenda, aim for a balance between the need for open sharing in the group and the need to meet group expectations. Again, the group agreement is the ideal place to start. If you've never created a group agreement, you should soon (Read more on page 40).

The ground rules for your group could include an option where the group can help a member process a life situation. Some issues involve more than a casual mention during prayer request time at the end. If a group member has faced a devastating turn of events like a job loss, marital blow up, issues with children, or other bad news, the group should allow space to sometimes put the Bible study aside and support their friend in need.

But, you don't want your group to turn into the "crisis of the week." While every group should offer support, there is a difference between a small group built on relationships formed around a Bible study and a true support group. If a group member needs dedicated support for marital problems, grief, or a life controlling issue, then a specific support group may offer better help (Read more on page 131).

There is no perfect way to organize every small group meeting. Your group can't offer only Bible study at the expense of care. But, your group also can't avoid Bible study and only focus on care. As Andy Stanley says, "This is a tension to be managed rather than a problem to be solved."

If during the discussion, you notice a group member getting teary or tender, stop and ask if they want to talk about it. They might or might not. The last impression you want to leave is that the meeting agenda is more important than the group members in the meeting.

When someone shares in the group, the response can't go to advice giving. They don't want to be fixed. They want to be heard. When others in the group chime in with advice, the person sharing quickly shuts down. Remember what your mom said about why you have two ears and one mouth?

Probably one of the worst examples of fixing happened in a group I lead in the early 90's. We were a group of six: one older couple, one younger couple, a middle-aged single guy, and me. During our prayer time at the end of the meeting, the younger couple asked for prayer because they were having trouble getting their one-year-old to go to sleep. She was often staying up until midnight.

The middle-aged single guy began to give them parenting advice. He had never been married. He didn't have any children. Yet, he was carrying on about how they should put their child to bed. We all sat there frozen. We didn't know what to say. Finally, after a few minutes he ran out of advice or at least words. It was the dictionary definition of awkward.

In a group meeting a few weeks later, I simply asked everyone to listen to each other's prayer requests without making comments. Our offender wasn't offended, and he obliged during prayer time. Fortunately for the group, that never happened again.

Group members need to feel heard. When people feel heard, they feel accepted. In a group, acceptance is oxygen.

Openness requires acceptance. Your group members are asking themselves, "If I share something hard, will the group accept me or will I feel embarrassed?" They aren't looking for helpful hits or advice. They want understanding. They want acceptance. They want the group to not act weird after they share.

Appropriate responses sound like "Boy, that must have been hard," or "I can't imagine how painful that would have been." What they don't want to hear is "My cousin had the exact same problem..." or "I know exactly how you feel." As much as we want to relate, none of us truly knows exactly how someone else feels.

The group should respond with enough so that the members sharing know that they are being heard. But, not so much that they feel interrupted or brushed aside.

If the sharer has a bad experience, he or she might leave the group. If she is a no show for the next meeting, it's important to follow up with her. You don't necessarily have to bring up the topic. Just let him know that he was missed, and you're looking forward to seeing him next week. If she admits feeling awkward in the group now, diffuse her concern: "Everybody in the group has gone through tough things. No one is judging here. We accept each other just the way we are."

Whether your group is looking for deeper Bible study, deeper sharing, or deep dish pizza, it's important to start with expectations of what the group should be. If your group is the place for your members to decompress from the worries of life, then make it a value to let it all hang out. If your group is longing for deeper spiritual things, then find an appropriate study, set the right tone, and remind the group of James 1:26-27: "Those who consider themselves religious and yet do not keep a tight rein on their tongues deceive themselves, and their religion is worthless. Religion that God our Father accepts as pure and faultless is this: to look after orphans and widows in their distress and to keep oneself from being polluted by the world."

But, remember, the pace of the group starts with you. Group members typically won't go any deeper than their leader. Take the plunge yourself, and your group will also go deep.

As you prepare for your first meeting, know that God is with you. With God's presence and power, you will have a great meeting. Be yourself. This gives others permission to be themselves.

Pray often. Delegate everything. Don't sweat the small stuff. You'll do great!

CHAPTER 4
SHARING LEADERSHIP

In my early days of leading a small group ministry, I felt the future and growth of groups depended solely on the ability of small group leaders to identify, recruit, and train an apprentice leader, who would eventually start a new group. My group leaders had a hard time identifying an apprentice. They looked at their groups and didn't see any potential leaders. By contrast, I looked at their groups, and recruited their group members for a leadership training group, where they spent six weeks with me, then were commissioned to launch a group on their own. I could find potential leaders in the groups, but the leaders couldn't.

I put a lot of pressure on my group leaders to find an apprentice. After all, the overall success of our small group ministry depended on the leaders training an apprentice. Things got pretty ugly. My leaders would pass me in the hall on Sunday morning and say, "I'm working on my apprentice." I wondered whatever happened to saying, "Hello."

After a long season of frustration, I gave up on the "a-word," apprentice. I announced to my leaders they would no longer need to worry about an apprentice. They cheered, hoisted me onto their shoulders, and marched me around the church building until the walls fell down. Okay, they just cheered.

Now that "apprentice" was a dirty word in our church, I introduced a new idea -- instead of training one person to lead, the group leader needed to train the entire group to lead. The cheering stopped, well, not really.

There are prospective leaders in every group, including yours. The best way to identify potential leaders is to let your group members try their hand at leadership. Shared leadership can range from bringing refreshments to hosting the group in different homes to leading the discussion (or part of the discussion). Everyone can do something. Everyone should be expected to do something. Put it in your Group Agreement.

Some of my leaders struggled with this. They would come back and say, "Well, I asked our group members, but no one volunteered."

I asked the leader, "How did you invite them?"

The leader replied, "Well, I asked if anyone would like to."

You see, there's the problem. If you ask people if they'd like to lead or help, then they have to consider whether they would like to remain comfortable in the group or choose the discomfort of trying something new instead. You can probably guess that the group members will choose comfort over discomfort. Are you surprised?

But, if you ask a different question, you get a different answer. Try something like "Today is the first and only meeting where I'm going to lead the discussion. I'm passing around the list, and everyone needs to sign up." That works.

By taking turns in leading different aspects of the lesson or the group, group leaders can easily identify who's got the stuff to eventually lead on their own. It's much easier to spot potential group leaders by seeing them in action.

How to Get Group Members to Lead

I am going to give you an honest answer. It's a very direct answer, but it's the correct answer. The answer is stop doing it for them. As long as you continue to allow your group to depend on you to host the group, you will host the group. If you give them the option, the group will always default to the easiest way: let the leader do it.

There are many good reasons to allow members to host the meeting in their homes or lead the group discussion. You know that members will take more ownership of the group with the responsibility of hosting. They will feel a stronger sense of belonging. By sharing responsibilities for the group, the attitude will change from "your group" to "our group."

There are potential leaders who need to have the experience of hosting or leading the group. It could be their first step toward leading a group themselves. Maybe you're just tired of vacuuming and straightening up right before the meeting. These are all legitimate reasons to let your group members host the group in their homes.

You're the group leader. You're not the group parent. Your members should sign up to bring the refreshments, host the group in their home, and facilitate the discussion. But, as long as you give them the option to stay at your house, eat your food, and let you do everything, they will.

In Exodus 18, Jethro had a conversation with Moses. He told Moses that doing everything for the people wasn't good. Why did Jethro think that it wasn't good? Because Moses' wife and children left Moses' home and were living with Jethro (Exodus 18:2-4). Moses gave his reasons for doing the work by himself: (1) I'm the only one that can do it and (2) the people like coming to me. You have to wonder how much Moses also liked doing for the people and having them come to him. Jethro gave Moses a strategy of how to lead without having to bear all of the responsibility himself. Moses delegated responsibility to other people, while overseeing the whole nation.

You don't have a nation to look over, but you do have a group to lead. Leadership is not providing everything for everyone and doing everything for them. Leadership is making sure that things get done and developing your members into leaders along the way.

Tell the group that you need their help. You don't need to tell them all of the reasons why. In fact, if you do, you're probably just giving them excuses for why they can't do it either. Affirm your group. Let them know that you love them. Let them know that they're important to you. Then, let them know that you can't do all of this alone. Even if the reason that you can't do it all anymore is that your members should -- that is reason enough.

Once you've announced that you can no longer host, then ask the group where you will be meeting next week. You may permanently move the group to another member's home or you might rotate the group to different people's homes. Once meeting at your home is off the table, your group will figure out where else to meet. The same goes for everything else – leading the discussion, bringing refreshments, leading worship, leading the prayer time, and whatever else needs to be done.

It might seem easier to do things yourself, but that doesn't mean it's better to do it yourself. You members need the opportunity to serve in the group. And, by meeting in each others' homes, group members can get to know each other in another way. Our living space reflects who we are. Homes don't need to be perfect. They just need to be inviting.

Discovering New Leaders in Your Group

Once you have everyone serving in the group, you can clearly see who's ready to lead, who needs more practice and experience before they lead, and who can serve the group in other ways, but probably won't become a leader. While these thoughts often invoke some fear of losing their groups, the reality is most groups don't last forever. There are those rare groups that continue on for 20 or 30 years, but most do not.

A typical group life cycle is about 18-24 months. At that point, groups should be asked whether they want to re-up for another 18 months or re-group by either forming or joining other groups. If your members are developed as leaders, then they can start groups of their own and include people who've been waiting to join a group. You will be a very proud "groups grandparent" when that happens.

You will find that some group members are reluctant to take on a leadership role. They may need to start out with a smaller leadership role. Ask them to start the meeting with the ice breaker question or lead the prayer time at the end of the meeting.

Give them a heads up the week before. As preparation for their turn to lead, ask them to observe how you start the meeting with the ice breaker or how you lead the prayer time. Even if they've been in the group for a year, it's a much different experience preparing to lead than it is to just participate.

After the meeting, debrief about the member's experience in leading. How did it feel? What did they feel worked well? What would they do differently next time? Give them the space to process their experience without jumping in and giving additional direction at first. Then, ask the group member if they would consider leading part of the meeting again in the future.

The member may do the same thing in a future meeting until they feel confident in leading the entire discussion. Be patient with them and allow them to develop at their own pace, but don't back off so far that they feel completely off the hook.

If you know someone is fully capable of leading the group discussion, but continues to be reluctant, then call in sick or call in busy 10 minutes before the meeting. Tell the reluctant potential leader that you can't make it, and you need them to lead the discussion that night. This is easier to do if the group is meeting in someone else's home. If the group meets at your house, then you'll have to go hang out at a coffee shop.

Remember, you called in busy. Show up before the meeting ends and debrief with the potential leader. Get their feedback. Encourage them. You want to keep them in the leadership rotation for the group.

Some group members will readily lead the whole discussion. That's great. The idea is to develop all of your group members and not just one or two members. If the group has the sense that everyone is expected to lead in some way, then they will.

There are many general purposes for small groups. Among them are fellowship and friendship, disciple making, gift discover and implementation, outreach and serving, and leadership development. As God works in your group members, he will call them to serve others and possibly call them to lead their own groups. Your job is not just to run group meetings, but to develop each of your members and to help them identify their unique calling. More on this in Chapter 5.

Designating a Co-Leader(s)

Every group member should be expected to serve in the group in some way. You want your members to develop their gifts and gain confidence in their ability to lead, a few members will rise to the top and demonstrate the ability to lead in a larger capacity. A co-leader can help you lead the group. If and when you begin to coach new leaders, your co-leader will be essential in helping you manage the group responsibilities, especially if you need to visit another group on the same night that your group meets.

Once you identify a group member who has what it takes to lead, give them several trial runs at leading. Once they've proven themselves, it's time to designate them as your co-leader. You want a person who is growing as a disciple and not just growing in knowledge. While no one is perfect, it's important to involve a member in leadership who is living out what he or she is learning. It would be a good idea to talk to your coach about your potential co-leader before you invite him or her to lead with you.

A co-leader provides built-in emergency backup. Everyone has one of those days when you have to work late or you have to beat a deadline or your kid gets sick. With a co-leader, you already have backup. While there may be a number of people in your group who could lead the discussion, your co-leader is always ready, willing, and able to help at the last minute. It would be a good idea to let them lead once in a while even when it's not an emergency.

A co-leader will benefit from the lessons you've learned. As a group leader, you've learned some lessons the hard way. Don't let those lessons go to waste. As your co-leader is learning the ropes of ministry, share your experiences and include them in the learning. When they make a mistake, help them process what happened and what they should do next time. You've learned more than you probably give yourself credit for. Share your knowledge.

A co-leader will share the ministry. In the Bible, the Apostle Paul had many ministry partners over the years. Timothy, Titus, Barnabas, and Silas among others were there to encourage and help Paul. You and I are no better than the Apostle Paul. Group leaders need someone in their corner to share the ministry.

After a meeting, you and your co-leader can debrief the meeting. As you evaluate how the meeting went and how the members of the group are doing, your co-leader will give much needed insight and perspective on the group. It might not be as bad as you think it is sometimes. After all, two heads are better than one.

A co-leader prepares for a future group. Eventually, your co-leader might leave your group. It's up to you to make sure that your co-leader leaves for the right reason. Leaders who are not tapped for leadership will ultimately find a place of leadership somewhere else.

One of three things will eventually happen to your group. Your group will grow to an unmanageable size, your church will grow and need new small groups, or you as the group leader will be unable to continue at some point. If your group becomes too large, your group will become a revolving door circulating members in and out until someone gives them another option. This isn't a good experience for anyone. As your group continues to grow, you must consider everyone's ability to share in the group and everyone's comfort in the meeting space. If your group feels crowded, they will stop inviting their friends. If your members can't get a word in, they will feel unloved. When numbers go up, care goes down. It's crucial at this point to address these problems with the group. While it may be uncomfortable, if the group is also feeling the pain, then they will be ready to consider some options. Your co-leader could take part of the group and sub-group in the same home for a while. As your group continues to grow, your co-leader or even you might start a new group. Then, both the existing group and the new group can feel the love and invite their friends again.

As your church continues to grow, more people will need a small group. Sure, new people can attend an existing group, but that creates a little weirdness for everybody. New people do better in new groups, but they can certainly join established groups too, if the group is willing to make the effort. Your investment in your co-leader can certainly pay off with them starting a new group. I've seen groups start new groups and in a period of just a few months see the whole ministry grow to 60 or more people. You could never accomplish that in just one group. And, by the way, the best coach for your co-leader is you, so you can stay connected even when you're leading different groups.

Sooner or later, life can get in the way of group life. Whether the leader is facing a circumstance that might keep them from leading, relocation, or something else, if there is no one prepared to lead the group, the group will disband. If you have developed a co-leader, the group can easily continue with your co-leader taking over the group. As John Maxwell says, "There is no success without a successor." The unthinkable fourth scenario: You have no co-leader. Your group stops growing. As the leader, you burn out. One by one your group members stop attending for various reasons. And, eventually, your group is no more. There are a lot of factors that play into this, but, hey, let's not go there.

As your group members serve in the group by sharing responsibilities, pay close attention to those who demonstrate leadership potential. After a fair test of their leadership abilities in various capacities, then consider approaching someone to become your co-leader. Both you, your group, and possibly a future group will benefit.

New and growing believers need some care and guidance. As they learn and grow, they also need additional responsibility over time. They don't need a co-dependent leader who wants to do everything for them, who never thinks they're ready to move on, and who needs to be needed. After a season of no more than two years, group members should be encouraged to lead on their own. Leaders often find a million reasons why this shouldn't happen.

Jesus gathered his disciples with the invitation to "Follow me." After a short season of training, Jesus sent them out to experience ministry for themselves. He gathered them back together and debriefed their experience. Eventually, Jesus died on the cross and ascended into heaven, leaving his disciples fully in charge of the church on earth.

Jesus provided an effective model for developing leaders. The Son of God chose to empower and release them for ministry. The pinnacle of this empowerment was Jesus' ascension into heaven. While he promises to be with us always (Matthew 28:20), the disciples reached a place where they needed to serve on their own. Your group members will get there too.

Jesus knew Peter was impulsive. He knew Thomas needed more apologetic research. Jesus knew the tension between

Simon the Zealot and Matthew the tax collector. Libertarians and Liberals don't mix well. Jesus knew Judas Iscariot wouldn't make it. He knew the good, bad and ugly of his small group members, yet he chose to empower them to serve.

If your group has been together for 18-24 months, someone is most likely ready to step out and start a new group. If your group is younger than 18 months, it's time to pass around the group responsibilities and see who rises to the top. Don't get stuck with old group members living in your basement.

CHAPTER 5
MAKING DISCIPLES

The Key to Making Disciples

Few disciple making strategies are as effective as one simple practice: obeying Jesus' commands. In the Great Commission, Jesus charged his disciples with these words, "Therefore go and make disciples of all nations, baptizing them in the name of the Father and of the Son and of the Holy Spirit, and teaching them to obey everything I have commanded you. And surely I am with you always, to the very end of the age" (Matthew 28:19-20). This passage holds the key to true disciple making, yet it is often overlooked. In the last phrase, Jesus states, "teaching them to obey everything I have commanded you."

Well-meaning believers over the years have attempted to follow Jesus' direction by teaching his commands in hopes that once people knew the commands they would integrate them into their lives and make significant life change. Sometimes this happens. But, the typical result is believers who know a lot of what Jesus' commanded, yet live their lives in frustration, shame, and disobedience.

The key to making disciples is found in Jesus' words, "teaching them to obey." This is not teaching the commands. This is teaching for the purpose of obeying Jesus' commands. There is a significant difference. Once a person's life is aligned with the commands of Christ significant growth occurs. After all, how can people grow spiritually while living in disobedience to Christ?

What did Jesus command? Before you write a dissertation on Jesus' commands and do a year-long study, the process for obeying God's commands is simple: find a command and obey it. As someone once said, "Delayed obedience is disobedience." Ready?

In Matthew 22:37-39, "Jesus replied: "'Love the Lord your God with all your heart and with all your soul and with all your mind.' This is the first and greatest commandment. And the second is like it: 'Love your neighbor as yourself.'" This is known as the Great Commandment. Jesus took all 633 commands from the Old Testament and summed them up in just two: Love God and Love people. Start here.

Loving God comes from surrendering to him with all facets of one's being: heart, soul, and mind. Some translations add strength. What one desires comes from loving God. Thoughts are surrendered to what pleases God. Passions and motivation stem from a person's love of God. God is loved through worship. God is loved by intentionally inviting him into your circumstances. I bet you can come up with many other ways of loving God. What can you start doing today to express your love of God?

This isn't necessarily a huge add-on to your already busy schedule. In the course of your day, how can you acknowledge God? How can you spend time with him? Maybe you could sing worship music in your car. Or, maybe you should turn off the music and talk to God as you drive along. During your morning walk or your workout, pray and spend time with the one who made you. Before you jump into a meeting, pick up the phone, or correct your child, whisper a quick prayer for God's direction. I'm not saying to do all of these things. The point is in the course of your ordinary activities, you can find small ways to put God first.

The second command is to love your neighbor as yourself. How do you love yourself? You provide for yourself with the basics – food, housing, clothes, warmth, and so on. You enjoy being encouraged and socializing with others. You know how to love, because you love yourself. How's your neighbor doing?

By neighbor, start with the people who live next door. Do you know their names? If not, get to know their names. Pray for them. When your neighbors are outside, make an effort to connect with them. You may reach a place where you can serve your neighbor or help them in some way. This effort is not necessarily to convert them, even though you might get a chance to tell them your story. You do this because Jesus told you to love your neighbor. By taking a little time for your neighbor, you are living in obedience to Christ's command.

There is a side to obedience that is not uplifting or useful in spiritual growth. That's legalism. Legalism usually dictates certain practices to do and certain practices to avoid. The practices themselves are not usually the issue, it's the thought behind them. The thinking typically goes like this: if I live in obedience to God, he will bless me. If I live in disobedience to God, he will judge me. Don't get me wrong, there is some truth here, but there is also some error.

By avoiding sin, you avoid the consequences of sin. I fully agree. But, sometimes by avoiding sin, people become proud and self-righteous. They feel better than all of the sinners out there. This is not loving your neighbor as yourself. In fact, this is a belief that you are better than someone else. In a human effort to avoid sin, you find yourself plunging right into sin. Believers are not called to issue final judgment on anyone (Romans 14:10). That's God's job. While believers must be discerning in a situation by sizing it up, this is solely for the purpose of loving others like you love yourself.

The biggest problem with legalism is the underlying belief that by avoiding certain behaviors, you can make yourself holy and pleasing to God. While believers must live their lives in cooperation with God, human effort is insufficient to truly transform a person's life. You run out of steam. But, here's the good news – God never said you had to provide all of the steam! "I pray that out of his glorious riches he may strengthen you with power through his Spirit in your inner being" (Ephesians 3:16).

By God's work in you and through his power, you are set apart -- you are holy. Holiness is not maintaining a laundry list of what one ought or ought not do. Holiness is being set apart for God's purposes. To love the Lord your God with all of your heart, soul, and mind. This is counter to the world. People in the world's culture live for themselves. They chase things that don't last in hope of finding fulfillment, yet they never find it. Why? If the things of this world could satisfy you, you would be satisfied. People are only satisfied when they surrender themselves to God and his ways. The power of God's Spirit will enable you to obey what Jesus commanded and make you a disciple. Transformation comes only from God and living in obedience and surrender to him.

How can a group effectively make disciples? If the group merely studies lessons, then you are adding to the problem by providing more information without the expectation to see the group walk in obedience to God. But, as the leader, you cannot require anyone to obey. You can, however, encourage your group members to obey.

End every group discussion by asking every member to set a goal for themselves or take on an assignment for the coming week. You don't tell them what to work on, you ask them, "What do you want to work on?" The group members will choose assignments from something that stood out to them in the discussion. Different things will hit different people at different times.

The assignment must contain three parts in order to be successful. It must be clear, reasonable, and accountable. The more specific the goal, the better the chance of reaching it. Generalities don't tend to produce much growth.

The assignment should be clear. "This week I will read my Bible for five minutes every day." "I will walk for 30 minutes three times this week." "I will pause to pray before facing any big decision or confrontation." "I will not put my garage door down if my neighbor is outside. I will go and talk to them instead." It's clear.

The goal must be reasonable. If a person wants more of God's Word in their life, then reading the entire Bible in the next week is an unreasonable goal. If a person wants to get out of debt, then paying off tens of thousands of dollars in debt in the coming week is unreasonable. For some people, getting up an hour earlier every day to do something is unreasonable. Choose a reasonable goal.

"I will read one chapter of the book of James every day this week." There are five chapters, so you can read it in five days. "I will create a budget to manage my finances and begin to pay extra toward my smallest debt with the money I have." These are reasonable goals.

In addition to being clear and reasonable, goals must be accountable. As a leader, this is where you wrestle with the tension of wanting to help people grow, yet being uncomfortable interfering in their lives. If your desire was to become some kind of dictator to order everybody around and direct their every move, then I hope you would be uncomfortable with that. But, when people join your group, participate in the meetings, confess needs, and set goals, they are inviting you and the group to interfere in their lives. If you don't, you are letting them down.

It's messy. Some people have complicated backgrounds or difficult circumstances. It isn't convenient. Sometimes things aren't easily resolved. You have been invited to enter into another person's life, into their mess, and this invitation is one of the greatest honors any other person can give you. You don't need to fix everything. You don't need to have all of the answers. You just need to be willing to get involved like the Good Samaritan rather than moving over to the other side of the road like the priest and the Levite (Luke 10:30-36).

The enemy wants you to hold back. The enemy wants you to not get involved. The enemy comes to kill, steal, and destroy, but when you offer yourself to be used by God in someone's life, God comes to give abundant life (John 10:10). Your willingness to love your group the way you want to be loved is a tremendous opportunity to change lives for eternity. God will help you. You only need to ask.

Once the goal has been set, then the group provides support and accountability to each member. This can be accomplished by choosing partners or triads (the member with two partners), who will check-in on each other during the week. This is to encourage each member, pray for them, and check progress – either successes or setbacks. (More on partners and triads in the next section).

More than anything else, after each member has chosen their assignment, they need to know that at the beginning of the next meeting, they will meet with their partner or triad in the group to answer a simple question: "How did it go?" Just knowing that someone is going to ask the question is motivation enough to meet the goal.

As your group members begin to move toward their goals and meet their goals with the group's support and with God's power, you will see lives transformed before their eyes. Bad habits will be forsaken. Good habits will begin to thrive. People who thought they were too far gone or trapped in secret sin will experience freedom and forgiveness. Your group will impact the world in ways you could have never imagined.

This sounds like a lot more than an invitation to turn on a video and pour a cup of coffee, but the reward of facilitating life transformation is highly rewarding. You might feel overwhelmed at times. This is when you lean into God. This is God's work. You don't need to carry the burden. You only need to offer yourself to God and allow him to use you. He will do the rest.

Supporting Your Group Members' Next Steps

As group members desire to see God work in their lives and to grow in their relationship with God, they will need support and encouragement from the group. There are just too many distractions in the course of people's lives, so they need help in maintaining focus. And, of course, any effort at change comes with a certain amount of resistance. Have you ever made a New Year's resolution? How did that go?

Significant change requires significant support. That support can be found in the group. If your group has eight or more people, then it's not really possible for the group leader to be the support person for everyone in the group. Even with the best intentions, follow up will probably not happen. What's more, if you use the group meeting for everyone in the group to check-in, then there will probably be time for little else in your meeting. You need to offer the support the group members want, but in a manageable way.

This is a good place to introduce partners or triads in the group. These groups of two or three people can check-in on each other during the week to encourage and support each other. You can form these partners or triads in a variety of ways, but here are some thoughts to consider.

Who do you want coaching you on weight loss – the guy who lost 80 pounds in the last year or the guy who would like to? You want the guy who has succeeded.

If someone wants to get up at 5:30 every morning to start a quiet time, they need someone who is up at that hour to give them a wakeup call for a while.

Your group might not even want to use the term "accountability partner." For several years, my group had "prayer partners." Two of us got together every other week to pray for each other. There was some checking in involved in the process.

Done the right way, accountability can be a good tool to strengthen your group and deepen their relationships with each other and with God. As long as you keep the "Why" ahead of the "What," your group could be well served with this.

The partners or triads can meet at a designated time during the group meeting for a weekly check-in and to discuss each group members' progress in the previous week. By having the conversation with a smaller number of people, everyone has adequate time to share and to be heard without being rushed.

Accountability has to be something that someone wants. And, when they express the desire to be held accountable, then the partners or triads must follow through. If they ask for it, you owe it to them. But, accountability only works when someone desires it.

Forced accountability is less like having a spiritual coach and more like having a probation officer. Since most group members aren't working hard to avoid incarceration, making group members accountable is a failed enterprise. The title of that book would be "How to Lose Friends and Frustrate People." This is not what you have in mind. Here are some things to consider in developing group member accountability.

First, why do you feel your group members need accountability? Either accountability works well for you or you've heard that it does. Whether you're starting a new habit or forsaking a bad habit, the help and encouragement of another believer can be a great support and motivator. If your group members are asking for accountability, that is a beautiful thing. If you think your group members need accountability that they're not currently seeking, well, that's a whole other deal. Proceed with caution.

Think about what led you to see accountability was a good thing for you. More than likely, this was a process for you. It wasn't a gut reaction. You thought about how accountability could help you. You thought about what would work for you. You thought about who would coach you. It took a little time. Your group members probably aren't there yet.

Give them insights into how accountability has helped you, before you form accountable relationships in your group. Just casually bring up accountability during the group meeting. You might even start with a praise during the group's worship or prayer time, "I am thankful for my accountability partner. This relationship has really helped me maintain (a consistent quiet time or kept me in the gym or whatever it was.)" You have to show them the value of accountability.

"But, this will be good for them. We need to just get started." Imposing accountability on unwilling group members will backfire in a big way. It will be about as popular as the Brussels sprouts you serve instead of brownies at your meeting. Your group members want to grow spiritually. You have found a tool that will help them get there. Now, you have to give them the "Why?" and not just impose the "What."

Next, ask what accountability your group is open to? Every believer is at a different place in their spiritual journey. In fact, no two believers walk identical paths. While Jesus is the only way to heaven, each person's background, wounds, victories, personality, gifts, and passions are very different. What works for one will not necessarily work as well for everyone else. One size does not fit all.

The only accountability that works is the accountability that your group members actually want. They may very well want to forsake a bad habit or develop a good one. Accountability may be the perfect tool to get them there. But, only if they ask for it.

Once your group members have bought into the concept of accountability, there is nothing wrong with asking the group members what they would like accountability for.

What accountability has the group agreed to? Your group has already agreed to some things that require accountability. Your small group agreement outlines each member's responsibility to the group. If your agreement puts the responsibility on your members to let the group know when they can't make a meeting, then they have consented to accountability in that area. The same with the other areas of agreement: confidentiality, active listening, etc. If someone violates something in the group agreement, then you should definitely ask them about why they broke one of the ground rules for the group.

When your group members ask for accountability, there are right ways and wrong ways to offer it. Some accountability comes across as coaching and encouraging. Other efforts at accountability seem condescending and defeating.

Accountability fails when it's conducted by an accountant. "Your goal was to exercise four times last week, but you only exercised two times. Now, you need to repent and pledge to do better next week." Yikes! It sounds like they'll be skipping the next accountability meeting too.

The Bible tells us that "love keeps no record of wrongs" (1 Corinthians 13:5). If the purpose of accountability is to confront the person with their failures, it's a failure. The nature of accountability can't be merely a ledger recording wins and losses.

Accountability works when it's more like coaching and less score keeping. If the member only got two workouts in this week, then the response should be: "Good, you got two in. What kept you from doing all four? How did you feel after your workouts? How did you feel when you skipped your workout? How can I help you this next week?" What are the reasons behind the success or failure? What motivates them? What de-motivates them? Everybody is motivated by different things.

Accountability partners need to know that you have their best interest at heart. When you offer accountability to someone, your prayers are significant. Your short voice mail messages or texts or tweets can encourage them daily. But, encouragement should be given in appropriate doses otherwise it can seem like a backhanded rebuke.

Identifying and Trying on Spiritual Gifts

God gives spiritual gifts to enable believers to serve others in ministry. "Each of you should use whatever gift you have received to serve others, as faithful stewards of God's grace in its various forms" (1 Peter 4:10). When you were saved, God extended his grace to you. In the original language of the New Testament (Greek), this is the word charis.

In this passage, Peter introduces a concept of grace that at first seems puzzling: "stewards of God's grace." The concept of stewardship typically applies to money or physical possessions, but here Peter applies stewardship to God's grace. Go back to when you were saved, who else was involved in that transformation? Often coming to Christ results from a conversation or teaching from someone like parents, teachers, pastors, friends, or Dr. Billy Graham. You came to faith as a result of that person being a "faithful steward of God's grace." But, don't been mistaken, salvation comes from Christ, not anyone else.

Peter also includes the means of being a faithful steward, "Each of you should use whatever gift you have received to serve others." Remember, the Greek word for grace, charis? The Greek word for "gifts" is charismata, or "grace gifts." When believers use their spiritual gifts to serve others, they are extending God's grace to other people. While people can cry out directly to God and receive his grace, more often than not a faithful steward using their "grace gifts" is involved.

The Bible states very clearly that every believer has spiritual gifts to do the work of the ministry. In 1 Corinthians 12:7, Paul writes, "Now to each one the manifestation of the Spirit is given for the common good." Believers are part of the body of Christ, the Church, and as such possess spiritual gifts for the good of the rest of the body.

Many people don't realize they have spiritual gifts. They need help to identify them. While many spiritual gifts inventories have been available over the years, a comprehensive ministry assessment like Network by Bruce

Bugbee gives a well-rounded picture of not only a person's gifts, but also how their personality, abilities, and passions influence their unique life calling (brucebugbee.com). A resource like this or one that your pastor would recommend can be tremendously helpful for your members to discover and deploy their unique gifts.

In addition to a resource like this, observing your group members in action is also a key tool in helping them identify how they are equipped to serve. For some the use of a gift comes so naturally to them, that they really don't see this ability as something special. They just assume everyone can do the same things.

One caution here: it's easy to confuse God-given abilities with spiritual gifts, which are supernatural in nature. For instance, if a person in your group is very organized and has a management job, you might assume they have the spiritual gift of administration. This is might not be the case. They certainly have a God-given ability, but is this a supernatural ability, a manifestation of the Spirit?

Spiritual gifts tend to appear in more unlikely places. One example is the author of this book who has the personality of Attila the Hun, yet God has given him the spiritual gift of pastor to tend God's flock. This is also a good example of God's sense of humor. (My wife says I'm being too hard on myself).

Unfortunately over the years, there has been some controversy over spiritual gifts and their purpose. Different churches and denominations take very different views on spiritual gifts. For the purposes of small group ministry, I would encourage you to examine what the key passages of Scripture say about spiritual gifts, especially as they apply to your group, and discuss spiritual gifts with your coach or pastor to receive your church's direction on gifts. Most of the Bible's teaching on gifts comes from three key passages: Romans 12, 1 Corinthians 12, and Ephesians 4. A comparison of these passages reveals some principles to keep in mind in your group.

These passages name 20 unique spiritual gifts. Other teachers will locate more spiritual gifts or summarize a smaller number of giftings. You can explore these other views at another time.

Below is a listing of gifts in the order they appear in the Bible. There is no significance or lack of significance of the order in which they appear.

Romans 12:6-8 – Prophesying, Serving, Teaching, Encouraging, Contributing to Needs, Leadership, and Showing Mercy.

1 Corinthians 12:8-10 – Message of Wisdom, Message of Knowledge, Faith, Gifts of Healing, Miraculous Powers, Prophecy, Distinguishing between Spirits, Speaking in Tongues, and Interpretation of Tongues.

1 Corinthians 12:28 – Apostles, Prophets, Teachers, Workers of Miracles, Helps, Administration, Speaking in Tongues, and Interpretation of Tongues.

Ephesians 4:11 – Apostles, Prophets, Evangelists, Pastors, and Teachers.

Again, spiritual gifts are supernatural abilities, not natural abilities. For instance, a message of knowledge is when a person knows something they could not have known in any other way. It's something God told them. Now, the proper way to use spiritual gifts is probably more important than discovering which gifts you and your group members possess. It's not always appropriate to say what God has revealed to you.

In his writing, Paul always balances the diversity of spiritual gifts with the unity of the church body. "So in Christ we, though many, form one body, and each member belongs to all the others" (Romans 12:5). Every member needs every other member. In fact, the purpose of the gifts listed in

Ephesians 4:11-12 specifically states, "So Christ himself gave the apostles, the prophets, the evangelists, the pastors and teachers, to equip his people for works of service, so that the body of Christ may be built up." Your group and your church need your gifts and the gifts of your group members.

Notice in this passage that pastors and teachers are called to equip the people for the ministry. So often, the pastors are hired to serve the congregation. This is a wrong perspective. According to Scripture, pastors are called to equip the congregation, so the members can serve. Once your group has discovered and embraced their spiritual gifts, inquire about how you can share the ministry with your pastor and share some of the burden.

The church should be united in Christ. Paul writes, "There are different kinds of gifts, but the same Spirit distributes them. There are different kinds of service, but the same Lord. There are different kinds of working, but in all of them and in everyone it is the same God at work. Now to each one the manifestation of the Spirit is given for the common good" (1 Corinthians 12:4-7). People with different kinds of gifts should use them in harmony with everyone else. Just like a general contractor would hire workers with different skills to build a house, they are working together to accomplish the same goal – a well-built house.

The body of Christ should also be united in essential doctrine. "For we were all baptized by one Spirit into one body – whether Jews or Greek, slave or free, and we were all given the one Spirit to drink" (1 Corinthians 12:13). "There is one body and one Spirit – just as you were called to one hope when you were called – one Lord, one faith, one baptism; one God and Father of all, who is over all and through all and in all" (Ephesians 4:4-6). While every believer may not agree on everything, they should agree on the things that unite them. While different churches will practice doctrines and sacraments in different ways, believers are saved by only one means – Jesus Christ. Every believer is equipped to serve by the same Spirit in the same body in unity.

The church should be united in purpose. "So that there should be no division in the body, but all its parts should have equal concern for each other. If one part suffers, every part suffers with it; if one part is honored, then every part rejoices with it" (1 Corinthians 12:25-26). These are great principles for groups as well as the church as a whole.

Your calling is not to outdo other believers, but to live life together. One member suffering is equivalent to the entire group suffering. If a part of your physical body was diseased and needed treatment, then most likely that illness would take a toll on your entire physical body. Groups are not meant to be an assembly of individuals who want to grow independently of each other. The imagery of a body relates the idea of interdependence and connectedness. Can you live in isolation and independence? Definitely. Can you thrive there? Probably not. You need every other part of the body, and they need you.

Just as a body, though one, has many parts, but all its many parts form one body, so it is with Christ...Even so the body is not made up of one part but of many.

Now if the foot should say, "Because I am not a hand, I do not belong to the body," it would not for that reason stop being part of the body. And if the ear should say, "Because I am not an eye, I do not belong to the body," it would not for that reason stop being part of the body. If the whole body were an eye, where would the sense of hearing be? If the whole body were an ear, where would the sense of smell be? But in fact God has placed the parts in the body, every one of them, just as he wanted them to be. If they were all one part, where would the body be? As it is, there are many parts, but one body

The eye cannot say to the hand, "I don't need you!" And the head cannot say to the feet, "I don't need you!" On the contrary, those parts of the body that seem to be weaker are indispensable, and the parts that we think are less honorable we treat with special honor. And the parts that are unpresentable are treated with special modesty, while our presentable parts need no special treatment. But God has put the body together, giving greater honor to the parts that lacked it, so that there should be no division in the body, but that its parts should have equal concern for each other. If one part suffers, every part suffers with it; if one part is honored, every part rejoices with it. Now you are the body of Christ, and each one of you is a part of it (1 Corinthians 12:12-27).

The body is interconnected. It functions well when every part functions at its best. Group members are very different. They bring different things to the group meetings and to group life. Some parts are easier to get along with than others. Other parts draw more attention. Some parts work quietly with no recognition. Every part is important, but no two parts are identical. In group life, no one is allowed to speed bump another believer. No one can say, "I don't need you." You may not understand why, but you will.

Years ago, a man joined my group. I wasn't really sure why he was there. He was already in another group. I don't mind if people are part of more than one group, but it really didn't make sense to me. Why was he in my group too?

One day as we were leaving the restaurant where our group met, he asked me how I was doing. Truth be told, I was having a pretty rough day, actually a pretty rough series of days. He said some things to me from his experience that really encourage me that day. I walked to my car no longer wondering why he had joined my group. God sent him to my group for me. Don't write off any member of your group. They are there for a reason.

While the parts operate in unity, they do not function identically. At the end of 1 Corinthians 12, Paul asks a rhetorical question: "Are all apostles? Are all prophets? Are all teachers? Do all work miracles? Do all have gifts of healing? Do all speak in tongues? Do all interpret?" (verses 29-30). The obvious answer is "No." If everyone possessed all of the gifts, then many people wouldn't be necessary, yet Paul strongly states that one part of the body cannot tell another part, "I don't need you."

God gives different spiritual gifts for different reasons and seasons. In his wisdom, God chooses who will receive which spiritual gift. Some gifts are very public. Other gifts are fairly obscure and function far from the limelight. This is not based on one's spirituality or maturity. It is purely God's decision.

Spiritual gifts are not the permanent possession of the recipient. Gifts can change over time. Remember, gifts are God's supernatural abilities. Different circumstances come with different abilities. Often gifts that were useful in one situation will be replaced by other gifts for another environment.

While gifts are given by God, they can be controlled and directed by the person who possesses the gift. After all, as Paul writes in 1 Corinthians 14, "Everything should be done in a fitting and orderly way." Activating a gift is not like the impulse to vomit. You can control it.

Gifts can be developed within the safe context of a small group. Groups are a great place to try out a member's abilities for ministry or practice their spiritual gifts. Since the group accepts each other, it is understood that taking new steps can sometimes cause mistakes. The group can help members stay on track with the use and purpose of their gifts. And, of course, the last thing any group wants is an abuse of gifts.

These three Scripture passages reveal the overarching theme of spiritual gifts – the motivating force for doing God's work is love. "Love must be sincere. Hate what is evil; cling to what is good. Be devoted to one another in brotherly love. Honor one another above yourselves" (Romans 12:9-10). Gifts are not given to harm others, but to build each other up. "Let no debt remain outstanding, except the continuing debt to love one another, for whoever loves others has fulfilled the law. The commandments, 'You shall not commit adultery,' 'You shall not murder,' 'You shall not steal,' 'You shall not covet,' and whatever other command there may be, are summed up in this one command: 'Love your neighbor as yourself.' Love does no harm to a neighbor.

Therefore love is the fulfillment of the law" (Romans 13:8-10).

Of course the greatest treatise on love in the New Testament is 1 Corinthians 13. Isn't it interesting that this complete chapter on love is found between two lengthy passages on the proper use of spiritual gifts: 1 Corinthians 12 and 14? I don't believe Paul added 1 Corinthians 13 to give the Corinthians a break from teaching about spiritual gifts. In reminding the Corinthian church the proper use of gifts, Paul chooses to place the qualities of love at the centerpiece of this teaching. Gifts were not given as a means to outdo each other. People with certain gifts were not more important than others. Among God's Church, a diversity of gifts was found within the unity of the body with everyone operating out of genuine love. This is what God intended – not chaos, confusion, or competition.

Love is the source of all genuine ministry. Otherwise, why serve another? Love is the powerful force behind all of the gifts. Love is the character trait that should be most desired. After all, if you lack spiritual character, how can you instill character in someone else? "Follow the way of love and eagerly desire spiritual gifts, especially the gift of prophecy" (1 Corinthians 14:1). "Be completely humble and gentle; be patient, bearing with one another in love" (Ephesians 4:2).

The last instructions regarding spiritual gifts in these passages speak to submission to God and to the authorities he has placed over believers. First, Christ is the head of the Church. "And God placed all things under his feet and appointed him to be head over everything for the church" (Ephesians 1:22). If for a moment you wondered if your part of the body was the head, I'm sorry that position is taken. Starting with Christ's authority, God has placed human authority over believers. "Everyone must submit himself to the governing authorities, for there is no authority except that which God has established. The authorities that exist have been established by God" (Romans 13:1-7).

Ministry requires submission and humility to Christ and to the Body of Christ. "Submit to one another out of reverence for Christ" (Ephesians 5:21). Submission to authority creates order. "But everything should be done in a fitting and orderly way" (1 Corinthians 14:40). As your group begins to explore their spiritual gifts, check in with your pastor or church leaders about your church's definition and use of spiritual gifts. Different churches have different perspectives on spiritual gifts. It is important for your group to practice what is condoned by your church's leadership.

While some may fear that the use of spiritual gifts can lead to error or confusion, the proper use of gifts involves the acknowledgement of the qualities of unity, diversity, love, and submission in the body of Christ. Within these parameters, gifts can be wonderful blessings to your group, your church, and your community. No ministry should limit its efforts to merely human ability. God uses those who make themselves available to him.

Serving Together as a Group

While often in a group care, connection, and application are emphasized, service is also an important part of group life. As both a way to live out what the group is learning and embrace a more well-rounded approach to discipleship, serving takes the group out of the meeting and into the real world of meeting needs.

A group leader came to me once asking about some obscure nuance of a scripture. I looked at this leader thinking, "Really? This is what your group is hung up on?" I told the leader, "I think your group needs a service project." He agreed. The end result of group meetings and Bible study should lead your group to where the rubber meets the road, not where the rubber meets the air.

Serving is important to both the one being served as well as those who serve. Giving in this way makes the group more like Christ. "...the Son of Man did not come to be served, but to serve..." (Matthew 20:28).

While individual members of the group can certainly find places to serve within or outside of the church on a regular basis, it's significant for the group to serve together. When a group serves together, everyone serves. If the group members are left to finding service opportunities on their own, then some might serve and some will not. By serving together, you put some positive peer pressure on those who are reluctant to serve.

Serving brings the group closer to God's design for his church. The early church, on its first day, began the practice that "All the believers were together and had everything in common. Selling their possessions and goods, they gave to anyone as he had need" (Acts 2:44-45). Some service requires financial giving. But, even if your group doesn't have many financial resources, you can certainly give what you have (Acts 3:6). Can your group lend a hand? Offer an encouraging word? Give your time and attention?

Your group can find opportunities to serve in your community. What non-profits, agencies, or schools could use your help? Is there a neighborhood that could use some sprucing up and encouragement?

What needs are they drawn too? Don't limit what your group can do to just this list. If you see a need in the community, then your group is officially commissioned to meet that need in whatever way you can. If you see a need, fill it. You don't need to necessarily ask your church's permission to do good in your community. If the need is larger than just your group, then consult with your coach.

At our church in California, there was a group made up entirely of middle aged folks who had been in church all of their lives. Most of the men were in the building trade. Financially, this group was blessed.

One member of the group confided in me that he had a bad attitude toward homeless people. "I grew up with nothing and made something of myself. If I can do that, then anyone can do that," he thought.

Our church along with other churches in the community committed to provide a hot meal every night of the week at an emergency homeless shelter. People were to prepare and serve a meal to the homeless.

At our church, people were only allowed to sign up to serve the homeless as a small group. Individuals could join a group, but groups had to sign up together. I knew that if individuals signed up, I might get six out of 10 group members, but if groups signed up, then I would get 10 out of 10 to participate.

Our church committed to bringing a meal every Friday night. That particular year, the Friday nights included Christmas Eve and New Year's Eve. I knew when my group would be serving, or so I thought.

Once the project was announced on a Sunday morning, every date on the list was taken within a hour. My group didn't even get a chance to serve. The group of builders and their spouses did.

After that group served their meal at the homeless shelter, the group member that confessed his low opinion of homeless people gave a different report. He took me aside and said, "I was wrong. When we were at the shelter serving the food to those homeless men, I began to look them in the eye. I suddenly realized that if circumstances weren't much different, I could have been on the opposite side of that line." As a direct result of that service project, that builder began to send his paid crews to San Francisco on Fridays to renovate a building, which would house a homeless shelter. Another Bible study didn't turn the light on for his guy. Serving with his group gave him a new insight and a new perspective that not only changed his life, but benefitted many who were in need. Disciple making happens in different contexts, not just in group meetings.

Your group can be used by God in incredible ways as you make yourself available to serve. Even seemingly mundane activities can be a blessing to others and to you.

Giving a Reason for Your Hope

Our oldest son was born at the University of California Children's Hospital in San Francisco (UCSF). He was diagnosed with a birth defect before he was born, so our local doctors sent us to UCSF for his delivery and subsequent treatment.

There were many complications to his surgeries. He fought infections. Many people prayed on his behalf. There were times that my wife and I really weren't even sure if he was going to make it. It was a desperate time.

I struggled not only with the reality of the situation and all of the emotional ups and downs we faced daily, but I also struggled with my faith. We believed God could heal. People around the world were praying for our son. The more we prayed, the sicker he became. This wasn't how it was supposed to work.

After 90 days in the hospital, he was well enough that we finally got to take him home. After being home for about a month, we began to notice some symptoms that alarmed us. We rushed him back to the emergency room, then he and my wife were transported back to UCSF with me following behind the ambulance in our car. We faced another month long hospitalization.

A few days into our hospital stay, our social worker at the hospital pulled us into her office. Her name was Stephanie. She checked in with us every day. She arranged for us to stay at the Ronald McDonald House. (I don't have enough good things to say about them). Stephanie had seen us on our bad days and on our worst days in the hospital. She and I had frank conversations about God and faith and healing. She was a great support.

On that day in her office, Stephanie looked at my wife and I said, "It's so good to have people like you here, because you have hope."

"Hope, I thought. This woman had seen us at the most desperate time of our lives, and she saw hope?" Our emotions were so frayed at times and so raw, there was no energy left to put on a Christian façade. We were merely surviving from day to day and whatever crisis that day might bring. We had no energy to be sterling examples of Christ.

Yet amidst our emotional upheaval and the daily turmoil in our lives, Stephanie saw something in us that was not produced by us. The hope we had in Jesus Christ shown through our lives despite the fact that we were in such a desperate place. She saw the hope.

Paul writes, "Always be prepared to give an answer to everyone who asks you to give the reason for the hope that you have" (1 Peter 3:15). As your group is serving others in your community, people will see your hope. As your group bands together and supports each other, people will see your hope. Even when they see the cars parked on the street outside your house on a weekly basis, people will see you hope. Your job, then, is to share the reason for your hope. The reason is Jesus Christ.

Many believers are intimidated with any mention of evangelism. Yet, Jesus called us to, "Go and make disciples..." (Matthew 28:19). People are sometimes fearful of evangelism because of how it has been presented to them. They needed to memorize a lot of verses and Bible facts. They were told they needed to understand apologetics and have the answer that would turn someone from skepticism to faith. While these things might be helpful, and there are those who certainly have a gift of evangelism, you and your group are only responsible to answer the hope question.

Why are you always smiling? Jesus. Why are you fixing up the neighborhood? Jesus. Why do you meet together every Tuesday night? Jesus.

The answer is similar to the blind man in John 9, "A second time [the Pharisees] summoned the man who had been blind. 'Give glory to God by telling the truth,' they said. 'We know this man (Jesus) is a sinner.'

He replied, 'Whether he is a sinner or not, I don't know. One thing I do know. I was blind but now I see!'" (John 9:24-25).

For every member of your group, they can confess, "Once I was far from God, once I was lost in sin, once my life was only about myself, but Jesus changed all of that. He can help you too, if you're interested." That's the spirit of the answer.

Your group is a safe place for people to tell their stories. Not only does story telling help the group get to know each other and understand each others' background and context, sharing stories of faith prepares the group for sharing their stories with others.

A great exercise for your group would be to take a meeting or two and ask each member to share their story of how they came to faith. You might ask people to write out their story in advance. It might be good to give them a time limit, or if you choose, just let the stories flow over the course of several weeks.

By being prepared and practicing their stories in the group, they will be ready to give an answer for the hope that's in them. They don't need to knock on doors or preach on the streets, unless God leads them to do so. But, as your group serves and gives, as people notice something different about you, you are prepared to share the reason for your hope.

Our son turns 17-years-old this year. He's had to deal with physical challenges over the course of his life, but he's 5 foot 11 inches and about 120 pounds. He's healthy. God answered our prayers.

CHAPTER 6
LEADING YOUR GROUP

Whether your group members know each other well or not, it won't take long for differences to pop up in your group. That's okay. If people were identical, some of them would be unnecessary. Rather than dreading the challenge of people who might rub you the wrong way, the group needs to embrace the opportunity to accept and appreciate people for who they are.

In some cases, the group just needs to learn to love a difficult person. But, this is not license for bad behavior. The group belongs to all of its members. As the group grows to understand each other, they also must behave in such a way that honors each other. Some potentially bad behavior must be curtailed in order to keep the group going. There is a balance between understanding each other and giving direction to the group. This chapter will help you navigate that balance.

Understanding Your Members' Personalities

People are wired in very different ways. Some of this comes from their family background, their life experiences (good or bad), their education, their opportunities or lack of opportunity, and so many other factors. But, at the center of each person lies a core personality type.

In this section we will refer to these types as Promoter, Planner, Producer, and Peacekeeper. I draw these from Vicki Barnes, author of *The Real You: Making Sense of Relationships* (Two Harbors Press, 2012) who has mentored me over the last nearly 30 years. Others have called these Sanguine, Melancholy, Choleric, and Phlegmatic. Gary Smalley, author of *The Two Sides of Love* with John Trent (Living Books, 2005), referred to these personality types as Lion, Beaver, Otter, and Golden Retriever. Whatever terms you want to use, the point is people are wired very differently. A basic understanding of your group members' core personality types will go a long way in understanding each other.

The Promoter

Do you have a group member who just exudes enthusiasm? Do they chase rabbit trails and pull thoughts out of left field during the discussion? You may have a Promoter in your group.

This Promoter behavior is modeled by the Apostle Peter. Impetuous and sometimes flaky, Peter was the only one who jumped out of the boat at Jesus' invitation to walk on water. When Jesus announced his coming death, Peter rebuked Jesus, "Never, Lord!" he said. "This shall never happen to you!" to which Jesus rebuked him right back, "Get behind me, Satan!" (Matthew 16:22-23). When the soldiers came to arrest Jesus in the Garden, Peter drew his sword and cut Malchus' ear, which Jesus quickly healed. Then, in the temple court, before the cock crowed three times, Peter denied Jesus. Yet there was another side to Peter's enthusiasm.

On the day of Pentecost, when the crowd thought the 120 in the upper room were drunk, it was Peter who stood up and explained, "Fellow Jews and all of you who live in Jerusalem, let me explain this to you; listen carefully to what I say. These people are not drunk, as you suppose. It's only nine in the morning! No, this is what was spoken by the prophet Joel…" (Acts 2:14-16). Peter's off the cuff proclamation that day resulted in 3,000 people being added to their number. There was no time to prepare a sermon. There was no time to create an outline. There was only time for a disciple empowered by God's Spirit to open his mouth and be willing to speak. This time Peter got it right.

The Promoter is the life of the party. In fact, a Promoter's motto could be "If you can't be with the one you love, then love the one you're with." Now, before you take that thought too far, a Promoter can have a great time with family and friends, but can also have a great time standing in line at the Department of Motor Vehicles. Promoters have never met a stranger and are easy to like.

They have an idea a minute, which lends to their impetuous temperament. Promoters are great starters, but poor finishers. After all, how can you take something to completion if you have an idea a minute? Before one thing is even half completed, they are chasing their next idea!

Promoters are great for adding enthusiasm to a group, rallying the troops, and recruiting new members. Promoters are not so great at staying on task, starting or ending on time, or maybe even remembering they are leading on a particular week. But, if you take a Promoter's idea, pass it on to a Producer to execute, and then add a Planner's eye for detail with the Peacekeeper checking in with everyone, your group can be a great team.

Be selective about what you delegate to a Promoter. You will see them as flaky, and they might feel frustrated. But, put them in their sweet spot of brainstorming and encouraging, and then you've got something.

The Planner

Do you have a detail person in your group? The one who catches typos and corrects any inaccurate dates? This is the Planner. The Planner personality is concerned with systems and order.

If the Planner had a motto, it would be "A Place for Everything, and Everything in Its Place." Planners choose careers from homemakers to attorneys to accountants to engineers. They tend toward perfectionism and are concerned about every detail. If you want to make a Planner's day, then give specific appreciation to the details of what they did. Rather than making a general compliment like, "You led a good Bible study," you want to get specific, "I really liked how you brought out the cultural background of that passage. It really put that Scripture passage in a whole new light for me." They will be thrilled.

Planners will follow the rules and probably add a few of their own. They may be determined to go through every question in a study guide, which is not really necessary. Just so they can sleep at night, the group leader should inform everyone that "there are too many questions to possibly cover in one lesson, so you have selected a few key questions to discuss." The group is welcome to explore the rest on their own.

Luke the Evangelist, who authored the Gospel of Luke and the Acts of the Apostles, represents the Planner personality. Luke was a Gentile believer and does not appear in Scripture until the middle of Acts when the pronouns change from "they" to "we" (Acts 16:10). Yet, Luke wrote a Gospel. In fact, he was the only Gentile and the only non-eyewitness to do so. This is where his Planner characteristics come out,

"Many have undertaken to draw up an account of the things that have been fulfilled among us, just as they were handed down to us by those who from the first were eyewitnesses and servants of the word. With this in mind, since I myself have carefully investigated everything from the beginning, I too decided to write an orderly account for you, most excellent Theophilus,　so that you may know the certainty of the things you have been taught" (Luke 1:1-4).

It's not that Matthew or Mark had done a terrible job. It's not that the Holy Spirit was absent from the inspiration and revelation necessary to pen Scripture. Luke, as a Planner, needed to thoroughly investigate things himself and share the conclusions with his disciple, Theophilus. While Peter couldn't sit still long enough as a Promoter to write himself, Mark wrote on his behalf. Paul, the Producer, didn't need to rewrite the Gospel. He was too busy breaking new ground. Luke took the time for careful research. He was a Planner.

Planners are going to, well, plan. They will plan an event. They will write an instruction manual for the event. They will write a dissertation on the manual for the event. They need to be given reasonable expectations and a deadline, then get out of their way.

Planners tend to be the least spontaneous of all of the personality types. They prefer to make a plan and stick to a plan. It will frustrate them to hear a constant flow new ideas, when the plan has already been set. Scrapping the plan is even worse. If they've worked hard and something has shifted, you need to take time with them and give them plenty of detail to justify　the　change.　Otherwise　they　will　feel　very unappreciated.

They can be accused of being nitpicky and critical. This mindset　can　often　lead　to　negativity　and　depression. Typically, Planners have low self esteem, so build them up. Planners wrestle with the mixed motives of belonging and contributing. They are pulled between thinking and feeling. They grapple with relationships and tasks. What they pour into a task demonstrates their regard for relationship, but they may become so absorbed in a task that the relationships are set aside.

Planners are wonderful gifts to groups and teams. The Promoter will get a great idea. They always have ideas. The Producer will be ready to execute, but will be short on the details. The Planner can turn the Promoter's vision into reality and help the Producer improve on what they are doing. The Peacekeeper is the most concerned that everyone is okay.

The Producer

A producer is known for being bold and drawn to action. The Apostle Paul is a great example. He was definitely a dynamic leader both for and against the church. A producer's biggest concern is power and results. Paul certainly had results.

Paul says of himself, "It has always been my ambition to preach the gospel where Christ was not known, so that I would not be building on someone else's foundation." (Romans 15:20). He didn't set out to thoroughly research and write his own account like Luke. Paul wasn't impetuous like Peter, the Promoter. He also wasn't trying to avoid rocking the boat like you will see with Abraham. Paul wanted to break new ground, fish or cut bait…you get it.

In a group, the Producer's concern will be over pace and results. They won't have a lot of tolerance for longwinded stories or discussions that go round and round with no clear conclusion. Now, please understand that even though this describes Producer behavior, it is not license for bad behavior. Producers can learn patience just like everyone else.

A Producer's motto is "get to the bottom line." In a group, the bottom line can be reaching the end of the study, taking on a group project, making a hostile takeover of another group so your group can grow. Okay, maybe not that last one.

Producers typically have the highest self-confidence and the lowest self-esteem. Their persona will be to charge any mountain, but in their minds they are only as good as their last accomplishment. When a Producer has a setback, they will try to "slogan" themselves into a positive attitude: "Our greatest weakness lies in giving up. The most certain way to succeed is always to try just one more time." (Thomas Edison) or "Failure will never overtake me if my determination to succeed is strong enough." (Og Mandino). Now there is some truth there, but as a group leader, realize that a Producer with a devastating setback is feeling it more deeply than they let on. Now, this isn't permission to start delving into their wound. They probably won't open up and share. But, their pain can certainly be exhibited in other behaviors like escapism, over-working, and certainly irritability.

Producers will help the group get things done. Sometimes Producers will get things done at the expense of speed bumping the relationships in the group. They will plow through a lesson to get to the finish, but may not pause long enough to discuss a heart break in one of the group member's lives.

If you want something done, put the Producer in charge, but maybe not in charge of the prayer time. Like all of us, Producers can learn and grow to become more like Christ. Jesus is working in them, even if it feels like you might be dealing with Attila the Hun. Remember Saul who became Paul on the road to Damascus.

Becoming a Christian doesn't give you a personality transplant. After all Dr. Billy Graham showed tremendous Producer behavior. Remember when he was challenged about his trip to Russia years ago? Someone told him Russia wouldn't accept the message of Christ. Dr. Graham replied, "They will when I leave."

The ambitious Producer nature of Paul's personality accomplished much for the spread of the Gospel. What can the Producers in your group help you accomplish?

The Peacekeeper

Do you have a group member who tends to get along with everyone else? They don't rock the boat, and certainly don't tip the boat over. They are loyal and steady. You can always count on them. Yet, you don't always know what's going on inside of them, because they wouldn't want to trouble you with that. This group member is the Peacekeeper.

Peacekeeper behavior is seen in several people in Scripture. The Apostle John would certainly fit in this category. He was the disciple whom Jesus loved. John had a warmth that resonated with others. He also took the longest to write his Gospel. While Matthew, Mark (writing for Peter), and Luke put out their Gospels in the first half of the first century (give or take), John's Gospel didn't appear until nearly the end of the first century. (Scholars can debate away, but this is what they taught me in Bible college).

Another example of Peacekeeper behavior is Abraham, formerly known as Abram. When Abraham had to go down to Egypt as recorded in Genesis 12, he was worried the Egyptians couldn't resist his wife, Sarah, for her beauty and would kill him to get her. Abraham instructed Sarah, "Hey, let's not make any waves in Egypt. Instead of telling them you are my wife, just say that you are my sister instead." Sarah went along. Now, this caused quite a bit of trouble later in the story when the Egyptians found out the truth. But, Abraham saved his neck.

When Abraham and Lot were living together with all of their families and herds, it became clear they needed more space. Rather than telling Lot where to move his family and herds, Abraham gave Lot a choice. Of course, Lot chose the best land. Abraham, being more passive, really didn't care which land he had as long as Lot was happy.

Now, no one is limited to one core personality type. Abraham's faith grew. God declared Abraham to be the father of many nations. When God called Abraham to take Isaac to the mountain and sacrifice him, there was no hemming and hawing. The next morning, they got up and went.

The Peacekeeper shows mercy and compassion. They are more likely to see all sides of an argument. Now, by seeing all sides, they sometimes have trouble taking sides or making a decision. I have a friend who asked me what color she should change her carpet to. I later found out she had been asking this question for more than a decade. The last time I visited her and her husband, they had moved to a different house. I said, "Well, you didn't need to change the carpet after all." Being a Peacekeeper, her response was, "Oh, Allen." If she'd been a Producer, the carpet would have been changed immediately, and she would have knocked my block off for saying something like that. If she had been a Planner, she would have studied carpet types carefully, and the science behind mood and its relation to color. If she had been a Promoter, she would have chosen whatever bright color she felt like.

Peacekeepers are natural mediators. They are slow to form a prejudicial decision. When Producers want to fire up their bulldozers and "git 'r done," the Peacekeepers are good people to check in with before the Producers start running over everybody.

Quite a few years back, another dear older friend and I were choosing a restaurant to take a group of senior adults to up in the Mother Lode near Sonora, California. There was an Italian restaurant there I had been wanting to try, but my dear Peacekeeper friend suggested something else. It was more of a coffee shop with an extensive menu. We went her way. At one point in the meal with about 40 of us gathered around a huge table, I heard her say quietly, "Isn't this nice? Everyone found something they really liked." She was a Peacekeeper extraordinaire.

While Peacekeepers are great listeners and mediators, they can be easily overwhelmed, yet they won't let you on to that. They may appear calm on the outside, but you may be rocking their boat like crazy on the inside.

When it's all said and done, we should all strive to be more like the Peacekeeper. In fact, as we mature and grow as a person, all four of these personality types should even out in our lives.

Understanding each other is an important factor in groups. Producers and Peacekeepers will always rub each other the wrong way. Promoters and Planners will do the same. When all of the differences come together, great things can be accomplished. But, if energy is spent trying to fix other people, not much will be accomplished at all.

For additional training on personalities types including an assessment, visit allenwhite.org/learn.

Keeping Group Conversations About the Group

Every group has a limited amount of time. Most group meetings last only 90 minutes to two hours. Keeping the conversation about the group is essential in accomplishing everything the group wishes to achieve. But, this is not just about the focus of the meeting content, it's also about the keeping the focus on the group members' lives.

When conversations move away from group members and go into other extended family matters, co-workers, neighbors, politics, or the news of the day, the group can become distracted from its purpose. You may protest, "But, isn't the group's purpose to care about people?" And, you would be correct. The group's purpose is to care about the people in the group and how life around them directly affects the group members.

Say for instance that in the group's prayer time, a group member requests prayer for his Aunt Gertrude's big toe. "She has always struggled with gout and bunions. This is time it is especially bad. Even though I don't see her very often because she lives on the opposite coast, I just can't imagine the suffering that she's going through…"

Honestly, it's terrible that anyone would have to endure such pain, but how is this situation directly affecting the group member. If Aunt Gertrude was living with the group member, and her condition was keep the group member and his family awake every night, then that's something to pray about in the group. If the group member is responsible for trimming the nail on Aunt Gertrude's big toe, again, a relevant issue. But, if the group spent time discussing every dilemma raised at the water cooler at work, every neighbor violating the HOA covenants, and every cable news report of something terrible in the world, the group could never get to what they need to deal with – growing to become like Christ.

Deal with – there's the issue. Sometimes group members bring up issues outside of the group as a smoke screen. They want to contribute to the group, but they don't want to disclose personal things about themselves. Instead, they talk about general things that take the focus off of them. They have the benefit of participating while experiencing the "safety" of not actually saying anything.

The discussion and the prayer time especially need to focus on what is directly affecting the group members. Your group doesn't need the news report. There will always be unrest in the Middle East. The economy will be up and down. Politically, party will always be against the other party. Tragic events will occur. The news never changes. But, if your group member is on the news, if the tragedy was local and involved someone whose life they touched, or if the economy has caused uncertainty about their employment, then those are things to bring up.

If a co-worker or a neighbor is struggling, and God has put it on the group member's heart to reach out to them, then, yes, pray about an opportunity to support or encourage the co-worker. There is a difference about what is directly relevant to the group and what is indirect or irrelevant. Keep the discussion focused on the group members and their lives.

This would be a good issue to discuss with the group and add to your group agreement (more on page 40). Every group member would understand what the group will spend time discussing and what they won't. This will also draw the line between prayer requests and gossip (more on page 124).

Your group members make time weekly to be a part of the group. As the leader it's important to guide the discussion away from general concerns about people or events outside of the group, and toward what is significant specifically to the lives of the group members.

Dealing with Overly Talkative People

After just a few group meetings, you will discover that there are some people that have a lot to say. They answer every question. They dominate the discussion. You secretly hope that they won't come back. But, the fear is that the rest of the group might leave. What do you do?

This is a tough one, because you want people to open up and share. Unfortunately, some people aren't self-aware enough to realize that no one else is talking and that the group is not all about them. I know this guy. I've been this guy. Here's how to deal with me, I mean, him.

First, take a deep breath. This isn't going to be the showdown at the O.K. Corral. Jesus is with you. He wants them to pipe down too.

Next, drop a hint. After two or three questions, if the big talker keeps chiming in and dominating the discussion, say something like this: "Okay, some of you have been kind of quiet so far, on this next question, let's hear from someone who hasn't shared yet." For most big talkers, this should work.

Don't look the overly talkative member in the eye. When you ask the next question, intentionally avoid eye contact with your big talker. Look at other people. Pray that they will open their mouths. By avoiding eye contact, you discourage the big talker from speaking up.

If the big talker still doesn't get it, then in the next meeting, intentionally place yourself right next to the person. First of all, this avoids direct eye contact, because you can't really do that without the risk of a neck injury. Secondly, if they haven't gotten the hint by now, when you ask the question and see him begin to answer, tap him on the leg or gently elbow him. This will cause him to pause long enough to allow someone else to answer.

If all else fails, then deploy what I call "The Nuclear Option." If after using these tactics for a couple of meetings, the big talker still hasn't changed, it's time to have "the talk." It goes something like this: "Have you noticed that some of the folks in our group don't talk very much? Would you help me draw some of those folks into the conversation? Here's what I need. Let's wait until a couple of our quieter folks have shared with the group before you jump in. You have some great things to say, but we need to make sure everyone has a chance to get their word in."

Here is what I suspect about your big talker. He or she probably has a leadership gift, a teaching gift, or a neurotic personality (I'm not joking). If she is a leader, then with the right coaching, she could probably lead her own group one day. She just needs to be directed toward the right behavior in group. If he has a teaching gift, then a class or another more formal setting would be better suited for his gift. Small group leaders with a teaching gift turn their group into a Sunday school class, even if they don't meet on Sunday.

If the person constantly talks about himself and completely dominates the discussion, even after you've exercised the Nuclear Option, then you might have a bigger problem on your hands. "The term 'neurotic disorder' is used to loosely describe a range of conditions that involve an inability to adapt to the surrounding environment'" (Source: Lifescript.com). This is the time to seek out your coach and other resources your church or community might offer. Your pastor or a counselor is a great resource to get advice on how to help a neurotic personality. Chances are your pastors might already know your big talker.

While small groups are a place to share and to support each other, leaders must be conscious of how the behavior of one member can affect the entire group. Work with your big talkers. Your small group will thank you.

Starting the Meeting On-Time

Lateness is a bad habit. While there are occasions when someone will run late once in a while, it is an exception. When you think about your group, the same people are consistently late. Once in a while, they may come early because they forgot to change their clock or something, but for the most part, they are consistently late. It's a bad habit.

If you want to reinforce their bad habit, then wait until everyone has arrived before you start the meeting. The latecomers will understand that the whole group will wait for them, so there's no need to be on time. If you want the latecomers to think about changing their ways, then start the meeting on time. When they walk in and the meeting is already started, they will say, "Oh excuse me, I'm sorry for being late." That little bit of awkwardness or embarrassment just might motivate them into being on-time next week.

Here's the flip side: if you wait for people who are always running late, what message are you communicating to the group members who show up on time? By waiting for latecomers, you are dishonoring the people who cared enough to show up on time. My rule of thumb is this: respect those who are on time by starting the meeting. The latecomers might continue in their bad habit, but more likely they will get there on time.

Welcoming New Members: A Little Small Group Weirdness

Adding new members into your small group is a bit like getting married and suddenly having in-laws. You know they're related to you, but that doesn't keep it from being awkward at first.

When a new person shows up, the whole group very quietly and politely freaks out. "Who are these new people? Can I share like I normally do in group? Will they repeat what they hear at the meeting? Why can't they find their own group?!"

To be fair, there is some freaking out happening in the other direction as well. "What is this group like? Will they accept me? Will they judge me? Will they think what I have to say is dumb?" Wow, with all of this going on, no wonder everyone wants to close their groups. Here are some ways to welcome new members and keep the freaking out to a minimum:

When new members join your group, it's a good time to review your group agreement. Every group should articulate their expectations. Whether they are written down or just announced, it's important to let new members know what is expected of them and to remind current members as well. Your group's ground rules don't need to be elaborate, but it should address things like when and where the group meets, confidentiality, childcare, starting time and ending time, listening rather than "fixing" especially during prayer times, and other things that are important to your group. You might want to include letting the group know when members have to miss. Also, if your group shared responsibilities, then let the new members know that they will eventually lead the discussion at some point, host the group in their home, or provide refreshments.

Make a special effort to fill new members in on inside jokes. Every group has a history. Things that happen over time become woven into the fabric of group life.

In a men's group I once led, just as the discussion was about to begin, the guys would ask "What about Bob?" It was a reference to the movie starring Bill Murray and to Bob, who was one of our original group members and who also happened to be a psychologist. Bob often got pulled into meetings at work and couldn't make it to the group -- thus, the inside joke. When someone asked "What about Bob?"we would stop to explain what we were talking about to the new group members. Once the new guy started asking "What about Bob?" we knew that he felt at home.

Be patient with new members. They will learn the rhythm of your group, if you don't scare them off. They will learn how long an appropriate comment should be. Does your group speak in sentences or paragraphs? Give them time, and they will get a feel for the ebb and flow of the group's conversation.

Adding new members can make everyone uncomfortable. The good news is that God never called you to be comfortable. New members mix things up a little bit, which is good for your group. They will question things including long-established practices in the group, which will make you rethink why you do what you do. That's a good thing.

People like routine. Groups can become uncomfortable when they fall out of their routine. Rather than scratch your head and wonder why you can't just get things back to the way they used to be, you should thank God for the continuing ministry of your group. After all, groups with no new members, eventually become groups with no members at all.

How to Stay Connected to Busy People

The pace of life can certainly interfere with group life. A wise person observed, "Today, people have more ways than ever to connect, yet are more disconnected than they've ever been." I would certainly agree. There is a big difference between things that keep us busy versus things that keep us connected.

What happens outside of the group effects what happens in the group. The time you spend with your group members outside of the group meeting will increase the quality of the group meeting experience. Typically, you would think of inviting group members to a cookout, meet for coffee, or even run an errand together. But, what do you do when they can't get together?

Call a friend. Busy friends probably don't have an hour to talk, but they might have a few minutes. Just call to let them know that you're thinking about them. A quick check-in to follow up on a prayer request or to let them know that they're missed means a lot to group members. Recommendation: It's best that male leaders call male group members, and females call females. You wouldn't want your concern to appear to be something else.

Pray on their voice mail. If you feel prompted to pray for one of your group members, why not let them know? When you call, even if you just get their voice mail, let them know that you are praying for them and their situation. You might even want to pray right there on the phone. It will especially mean a lot to let them know you just called because you care, and that's it. If you add on two or three reminders, questions, or other information at the end, they might wonder why you really called. Suggestion: This works great on personal voice mail, but not so great on a home answering machine. Just imagine if someone else in the house hears a message that says, "I am praying for you and the difficulties you are having with your spouse..."

Written communication, including email, is far more difficult than in-person or even voice communication. Emails lack tone of voice and attitude. If you emailed, "Glad you could make it to group last night," what did you intend to say?

A. I was glad that you were there.

B. Even though you were very late, I'm glad you could make it.

C. Even though your attendance has been very erratic, I'm glad you could grace us with your presence.

D. I feel like the group is a very low priority to you, so...

You get the picture. Email can help us stay connected, if you know a person well, and if you are very clear with what you mean. Caution: Never try to resolve a conflict via email. It will turn into a nightmare. Even if someone shoots you an angry email, ask when you can meet face to face to discuss the situation. If you write an email in response to a conflict, push "Delete" not "Send."

While Instagram, SnapChat, Twitter, Facebook, Texts, and other social media tools can be overwhelming, they can also help you stay up to date with your group members. Again, the same cautions apply as with email. It's not the same as a conversation over coffee, but sometimes a short text is better than nothing.

I started a men's group over a decade ago. Our group met for lunch every Wednesday and changed restaurants every month. I sent out a reminder every week about our meeting as well as to remind them of where we were meeting. Every week one group member, David, would reply to the email telling me what part of the world he was in and that he wouldn't make it.

David was a medical recruiter, so every week he was at a medical convention somewhere – Las Vegas, New Orleans, Minneapolis, New York City. I would reply and ask how he was doing and if there was anything he needed prayer for. He would always reply back.

Fast forward, I ran into David at the mall not long ago. He changed positions with his company and no longer traveled. Now, he regularly attends the group I started way back when but no longer lead. David said I should check out a group meeting sometime. That made me smile.

Just a small touch with a weekly email exchange kept David enough in the loop that years after I turned the group over to a new leader (and he turned the group over to the current leader), David felt enough connection that he rejoined the group meetings as soon as he could.

It's great to get everyone together, but sometimes that's hard to do. While these other means of keeping contact are not as good as a group meeting, they just might help your group stay connected with busy people.

Time Management in Group Meetings

A good group meeting can last anywhere from 90 minutes to 2 hours, but even with that amount of time, groups sometimes don't have enough time to discuss everything they would like to. If your group is meeting on a weeknight, your members will need to get up early the next morning for work and school. How can group members have adequate time to connect, yet get home at a reasonable hour. Let's get to the reason for longer meetings and see if there is a solution.

1. Your group might be too big. If your group has more than eight people, it's no longer a "small" group. Usually when a group grows to be larger than eight, the more vocal folks take over and the less vocal folks hide. The easy solution here is to sub-group during the discussion. This doesn't mean your group has to split up.

Sub-grouping can be as simple as creating smaller circles of 3-4 people for part or all of the discussion, then coming back at the end of the study to conclude the meeting. Another effective method is to have group members discuss the question with one other person, then share their discovery with the rest of the group. In educational circles, this is known as "neighbor nudging." Either of these methods can get your whole group talking and keep the meeting moving along.

2. Your group might be trying to cover too much. A good group discussion doesn't have to cover every question in the study guide. In fact, some of the best discussions might only touch on five or six questions. The strength of your discussion will be the thoughts of your group members based on the Bible and on their life experiences. As your group gets to know each other, it won't take as much to get them talking. Use the lesson as a tool to facilitate discussion, not a referee to rule the discussion. You'll need to keep things on track, but that doesn't mean covering every question in the book. You might even need a couple of meetings to complete one

lesson. Or, you can just cover the gist of the lesson and move on to the next.

3. Your group might be prone to chasing rabbit trails. While there is a place for catching up with each other, when it comes to the Bible discussion, the leader's job is to keep the discussion on track. If your Bible study on the character of being a good friend leads to a discussion of the end times, you're group is off track. The leader can just simply say something like "Well, we've certainly opened a can of worms here. Let's get back to biblical character" or "We'll need to save that topic for another day." Then, move on to the next question. Discussions that meander and frequently get off topic can become frustrating to your group members. Sometimes people don't even know how to stop the rabbit trail and get back on track. A gentle reminder from the leader and a move toward the next question often does the trick.

4. Your group might have a big talker. If someone is dominating the discussion or is answering every question, the leader needs to step in for the sake of the whole group. For more ways to manage a big talker, go to page 100.

5. Your group might not be spending any time together outside of the group meeting. What happens outside of the meeting will greatly influence what happens in the meeting. Service projects, block parties, prayer partner meetings, or even a cup of coffee between members will help your group become better connected. This will provide a less formal opportunity for conversation and relationship. These "meetings between the meetings" offer some needed relationship building so that everything doesn't have to happen during the small group meeting.

There is an art and science to group discussion. Leaders should avoid legalistic rules of discussion, but should also avoid the extreme of "anything goes." Finding the right balance for your group is something that needs to be fine tuned weekly. Sensitivity to the Holy Spirit and to your group members will go a long way in directing your discussions.

Handling Inconsistent Attendance

Every group faces ups and downs in attendance. A core of group members will attend every meeting without fail. Some members will attend more infrequently. New members will sign up for your group. Some will join. Others won't show up. When it comes to inconsistent attendance there are a few things to keep in mind as the leader.

First of all, it's not about you. In the church, community is what people want, yet it's what they resist the most. People got excited. They sign up for your group at church on Sunday. Then, life just gets in the way despite your best efforts to remind them and encourage them to attend. You did your best to include them. They just weren't ready to get there.

Keep them on your list. Keep the communication flowing. Email them along with the rest of your group. Give them a call. The call should go something like this: "Hey, I was just wondering about you. Is everything okay? I'm not calling as the truant officer. I'm just calling because I care." Chances are that they won't slam down the phone after saying, "I don't want you to care about me."

Focus on who showed up rather than who didn't. One small group I led had four people who regularly participated with another five or six on the list. One week, there were only two of us. By the numbers, my group might be looked upon as a complete failure. Yet, there are things you can talk about with two that you can't discuss with eight. Maybe you do the lesson. Maybe you set the lesson aside. Before you start beating yourself or your group members up over low attendance, you need to do a quick check-in with God: "God, what do you intend for this group meeting? It doesn't look like what I planned. What have you planned?" God's plans are better anyway.

Remember your small group and the ministry of your group are not the same. Some people may never show up for your group. Or, they'll come once or twice, then you won't hear from them for a while. Here's the deal: whether they attend every week or once in a blue moon, they are yours. The group members who meet three out of four times a month are essentially your small group. Everyone else is the "ministry" of your small group. There is a reason that God has placed these folks in your life. Keep up with them. Help them when they need help. Pray for them. This is not some clandestine plot to convince them to rejoin the group. This is your opportunity to serve, even if you never get anything in return.

In a perfect world, everyone would honor their commitment and show up for every group meeting. But, this is not a perfect world. Keep in mind that you just might be the only connection to the body of Christ for that flakey person on your list. Their well-being, of course, is not up to you. But, there is a reason that in all of the small groups in all of the county, they signed up for yours. God will show you why.

Low Attendance Could be an Opportunity

Every small group has fluctuating attendance. Sometimes everybody's there. Sometimes there are just a few people. You could easily launch into how uncommitted people are and scold them for being so irregular, or you could take another approach.

God arranges for every small group meeting to suit his purpose. Sure, you might be disappointed that you didn't have a full house, but sometimes what God wants to do can't be accomplished if everybody showed up. Rather than beat yourself up for being an inferior leader or beating up your group for being uncommitted, ask God what he intends for the group that day. Whether large or small, God has a plan for it.

A member of my small group was discouraged over some disappointments in his life. We had made several attempts to get together, but our busy schedules kept getting in the way. Then, one day at the group meeting, there were just the two of us. God had arranged for us to finally have our lunch. We had a great discussion, but it wouldn't have happened with the whole group present.

I know another leader who thought their group meeting just wasn't going to happen. Throughout the day, every member of the group called to cancel for that night. Eventually the leader's husband called and said that he was working late and wouldn't be there either. The leader thought, "Well, I guess I've got the night off."

At 7 p.m. the doorbell rang. The leader opened the door and was greeted by a couple who rarely came to the group. She had forgotten about them. Tempted to tell them that the group was cancelled and return to her relaxing, she thought better of it and invited them in. As the couple shared their story, the husband expressed his need for Christ. The leader explained what it meant to follow Jesus, and that night the man was saved. What if the leader had called off the meeting and turned the couple away?

You never know what God has in store for your group. Even when you have a full house, you need to ask God what he has in mind for your group meeting. It may be caring, sharing, praying, and eating. But, it may be something else.

How Big is Too Big for a Small Group?

One group in a series had 30 people meeting at their house. Is this legal? Will the small group police be visiting soon to split up the group? Here are a few tips for when your group attendance exceeds your expectations.

If your meeting space is large, then try to make folks as comfortable as possible. Just like a church auditorium, however, your room will only comfortably fill to 80 percent of capacity. If people sense that you have plenty of people in your group, it may become their excuse to back out of group.

Make sure everyone feels like they have a place and that they are welcome to the group. Remember, community is what people need the most, yet resist.

If your space is too small, do the best you can on week one, then develop a strategy for the next week. If you're using a video-based curriculum, crowd in the best you can to watch the video, then sub-group for the discussion. If you have a co-leader in the group or basically anyone with a clue, you might ask if part of the group could meet at their place next week. If that person is not readily apparent, then just ask the group: "It's obvious that we have a problem. Would anyone else be willing to have part of the group meet at their place?" Chances are that if most of your new recruits were just looking for a group in the neighborhood, they won't be offended by meeting somewhere else. They aren't attached to you yet.

Make sure everyone can get their word in. Any group larger than eight people (six in a restaurant) makes it difficult for everyone to talk in the group. In a larger group, a handful of the more boisterous members will tend to take over the group while the more timid members might not say anything. Have everyone crowd in to watch the video, then say, "Okay this half of the room will move to the living room, dining room, whatever you have available. The rest of the group will stay here." Notice that I didn't say, "Men, go in there. Women, stay here." Your group, most likely, won't stay at 30 people for the long term. Sub-grouping could lead to starting a new group down the road. Unless you want to intentionally start a men's group and a women's group, it's best to sub-group by couples in a couples group.

Quickly locate potential leaders. Once the group has sub-grouped, you can either ask for a volunteer to lead the discussion, or you can just see what happens. The leader will naturally rise to the top. Once, I heard a small group leader who had 45 people show up at their house for their first meeting. They used every conceivable room in the house to sub-group. Then, they asked the person in each sub-group with the most speeding tickets to lead the discussion. They were the risk takers.

Andy Stanley says, "if it has a back row, it's not a small group." Andy is a wise and intelligent guy. But, I also know that some folks have a wonderful gift of inviting and including others. Invite as many people as you'd like, but sub-group when you have more than eight.

Open or Closed Groups

There are good reasons and bad reasons to close your small group. One good reason to close your group is when a study becomes intensely personal. As your group is working through difficult issues in the lives of its members, it would be pretty awkward to add a new member. Once the issue is worked through, then it would be time to open your group again.

Your group could also be in a situation where a member of your group is facing a crisis. Rather than focus the group's attention on welcoming new members, for a season, the group needs to focus on caring for the member in need.

Then, there are some wrong reasons to close your group. For instance, the group is happy with the members they have, and they really don't want any new people to spoil the party. The group's motto is "We seven going to heaven" or "Us four and no more." The group may go on for a while, but the problem comes when a few members can't meet any more. As the group begins to decline in members, it becomes increasingly difficult to add new members, because the group has been so close-knit and tight for so long.

Another bad reason to close the group is fear that once a group reaches a certain number, the group will be asked to start a new group. Everybody's happy together. Nobody wants to leave. The thought is just to close the group to new members and avoid the problem. But, this only leads to other problems.

A closed group can easily become sort of a cul-de-sac. They are receiving, but not giving. Just as the Dead Sea in Israel has no outlet and continues to build up mineral deposits, groups can calcify and become not just stagnant, but also rigid. One solution to this is for the group to serve together. Whether your group serves a neighbor or partners with a service organization, your group has an outlet for ministry.

One of the worst things that can happen to a group is that the group just becomes all about itself. The group loses its edge. Everyone becomes more understanding of each others' behavior and less likely to confront bad behavior. It's easy to slip into complacency. A continued inward focus is not healthy for any believer or any group.

There are some good reasons to close your group for a season. There are also some good reasons to open your group:

First, you have the opportunity to help people connect who might otherwise be lost in the crowd on Sunday. People with friends in the church are the most likely to continue participating. Those who don't know anybody are much more likely to leave.

Next, an Open Group has the opportunity to reach people for Christ. While your group doesn't need to hand out tracts on the street corner, your group can model Christ for someone who is searching. Eventually they might cross the line of faith.

Open Groups make you more like Christ. I'm not saying that Closed Groups are ungodly. There are good reasons to be closed. Open Groups, however, can move you out of your comfort zone. Your group has to sacrifice something for the sake of another person. It takes extra effort to welcome new people and to help them fit in with the group. Open Groups force you to be selfless. It's not about what you like and who you like, it's about God using the group to minister to others.

Open or Closed really depends on where your group is and what you're called to accomplish. Think about these reasons and pray about what your group should do next.

What If Visitors Don't Come Back?

Group leaders get excited when new people want to join their groups. You roll out the red carpet and give them a warm welcome. New members bring a little excitement and a breath of fresh air to your group. You might even feel that your group is really starting to turn into something. And then, the new person doesn't show up next time. You might feel a little jilted. The first meeting seemed to go well. What happened?

It's not about you. As a leader, it's easy to feel a little rejection when a new member doesn't come back. I faced a little of this feeling back when I led one of my first groups. It was a men's group that met at 6 a.m. every Tuesday morning, and I am not a morning person. Some weeks we would have 8-10 guys. Some weeks we would have two. One week we had 18, but that was the week that my dad was visiting. I suspect that someone made a few calls for that one. What I had to realize was the attendance in my group had more to do with 6:00 a.m. than what I was teaching. After all, my lessons came straight from Chuck Swindoll. The lessons were great, and it wasn't me. Absences are not a reflection on your leadership.

Real life can quickly edge out group life. Things happen. Kids get sick. Sometimes people have to work late. Sometimes people are just tired. It's important to follow up with new group members, and let them know that they are welcome. If they've missed a meeting, give them a call to let them know they were missed or give the responsibility to a group member to make the call, just make sure the call is made. Their absence could turn into an opportunity for prayer or for your group to help the new member. It's hard to put yourself aside, as the leader, and pick up the phone sometimes, but remember this is not about you personally.

New habits are hard to create. If your new members have never been part of a group before, it takes time to develop the new habit of group life. Even after the new members have attended for a few weeks, the busyness of life might start getting in the way again. Remember, that most New Year's resolutions start fizzling out around mid-February. This same pattern can be true for starting a new group too. Your encouragement is just the thing that might help them to continue.

Don't read them through your lenses. Your new group member is not you. As the leader of a small group, you highly value group life. It would be a pretty drastic thing for you to stop coming to the group. Maybe you can't even think of a reason why you would ever forsake your group. But, your new group member is not you, so you need to avoid interpreting their actions through your point of view. Think about this, if a Planner (or melancholy) person thought through all of the pros and cons of attending or missing a group meeting, their absence would reflect their careful consideration. Their actions would be deliberate and intentional. If a Promoter (or sanguine) heard about a party as they were leaving work, and decided to join their co-workers rather than go to a Bible study, they wouldn't think twice. People who fly by the seat of their pants don't understand people who iron their pants, and vice versa. Your group member could very well be wired much differently than you are. (For more on Personality Types see page 75).

If the devil can't make them bad, he'll make them busy. Satan is an enemy of group life and an advocate of isolation. The less encouragement that believers experience, the greater his chances are to win out in their lives. How do you address this? You pray for your group members. After all, "greater is he that is in you than he that is in the world" (1 John 4:4). Your group is about spiritual things. Don't be surprised to encounter a spiritual battle now and then. But, remember, you and your group are on the winning side.

Assume that your new member didn't stop coming for the same reasons that you would stop coming. It's not that they are uncommitted. It has more to do with being new to group life and having yet to bond with the group. Rather than worry about the effectiveness of your leadership or the quality of your group discussion, talk to your group member. Maybe they are uncomfortable discussing personal things in a group. Maybe they misunderstood a comment someone made. Maybe they just need a little encouragement. As the leader, put yourself aside, as hard as that is, and follow up with the absent member. It just might be the nudge that they need.

Worship in a Small Groups

Worshipping together in a small group conjures up a lot of awkward memories. Even if you find a guitar player, few people sing, and no one sings very loud. The discomfort usually causes groups to abandon further attempts at worship. But, if you want to have a well-rounded group, how can you successfully worship?

First, you need louder music. Seven people sitting in a circle trying to sing along with an acoustic guitar spells disaster in most groups. A few people barely sing. If you know the words, you close your eyes or look down at your shoes. If you don't want to sing, you just pray that the music will end soon.

Worship videos can be a good alternative. The videos usually have the words and a visual, so everyone can look at the TV rather than working hard to avoid eye contact. The key is to turn up the volume. If you want your group to sing, the music needs to be loud enough, so people don't feel self-conscious.

Two or three songs are sufficient to focus the group away from the worries of their day and into the presence of God.

The group may not be into it initially, but they will discover that this is a great transition from the outside world to the group.

Think about this -- music is only one form of worship. Worship in a group can be built around methods other than music. You can read a Psalm with instrumental music playing in the background. Someone could read a poem. The group could write their praises on helium balloons and release their balloons to lift up praise to God.

Once I planned to open a small conference using worship videos. Unfortunately, the videos didn't work. So, we worshipped with Alphabet Praise. I called out each letter of the alphabet, and everyone chimed in with something they were thankful for or a word describing God's character that began with that particular letter. I warned the group ahead of time that the letter X was coming. I was afraid we would have to skip that one unless someone was really into xylophones. A woman in the back exclaimed, "X-rays that show my cancer is gone." I'm glad we didn't pass on X.

Celebrate communion in your group. Communion is a symbol of what Jesus did for us. Since communion is a symbol, you don't need silver trays or wafers that taste like Styrofoam. You simply need bread to represent Christ's body and a drink to represent his blood. Any kind of cracker or even matzo would serve the purpose. For the drink, you should err on the side of caution and go with something non-alcoholic.

The practice of communion is as easy as reading directly from 1 Corinthians 11:23-26. You can offer prayers or not. The important thing is to remember Christ's work on your behalf and in your lives.

My favorite communion elements are a loaf of French bread and bunch of grapes. Each person takes a hunk of bread and several grapes and shares communion with other people in the group. Sometimes this becomes the time to repent of an offense and to seek forgiveness. Often it's a time to encourage each other and to share appreciation.

Before you plan communion for your group, check in with your pastor or coach. There are many different views of the Lord's Table. Your group should practice what is in line with the beliefs and practices of your church.

Give a group member the worship responsibility. As the small group leader, your plate is pretty full already. Who in your group would be interested in leading the worship portion of your group? Has anyone asked about having worship in the group? Rather than trying to figure out how you are going to accommodate a request for worship, why not ask them to head it up?

Worship as a group at a church service. The easiest place to worship together as a group is during a weekend service at church. Rather than attempting music in your group, why not have the "professionals" lead your group in worship? It's a great group dynamic to attend the same service and sit together. This also encourages your group members to attend the services.

Worship in a group can be tricky, but it's not impossible. By asking someone to champion worship in your group and trying different ways to worship, your group will grow in enjoying worship together.

CHAPTER 7
SETTING GROUP BOUNDARIES

Leading a group brings the responsibility of guiding the group and its meetings. Groups are a great place to belong and to openly share in an accepting environment, every group needs some guard rails to keep things headed in the right direction and fulfill its purpose as a healthy group. Your Group Agreement (see page 40) will go a long way in establishing the ground rules for your group, but there are things that come up from time to time that need to be addressed. If these things go unaddressed, then your group could become unhealthy. Remember, leaders are the people who do things that other people refuse to do. Let these thoughts guide you as you lead your group.

Keeping the Discussion on Track

It's certainly easy for discussions to get off course and maybe never come back to the topic. This is part of the challenge of leading adult learners. Adults already have a lot of information and a lot of experience. Think of the brain as a filing cabinet or a hard drive. When you receive any new information, you open a file in your head with that label only to discover that there are other things in the file.

Let's say your small group is discussing Daniel and his vegetarian diet from Daniel 1. The group members' brains automatically open their mental folders for "Diet." While they're in there, they remember several diets that they've tried and failed at in the past. "Does anyone remember the grapefruit diet?" "How about South Beach?" "How about the tomato and cabbage stew diet?" And, off they go. Now some have cross-referenced from "diet" to "hunger." They're thinking "I wonder who brought the snack tonight. I hope it's not one of those Atkins dieters who only bring pork rinds..." Suddenly your group has traveled a long way from Daniel and Babylon.

You really can't stop adults from being distracted by their thoughts and experiences. It's just how they're wired. But, you can prevent this from becoming an epidemic in your group. If your group is fairly new, you can find some tips on keeping the discussion on track on page 120.

If your group has been around for a while and has formed this bad habit, it might be time to check in with the group and make sure everyone is okay. You might even be losing group members if this is going unchecked. Simply ask the group if everyone is doing okay. You might even add: "Permission to speak freely." Get the group to come to an agreement about staying on topic and socializing at the end of the meeting.

Sometimes you have to walk a fine line. When someone begins to go off topic, be careful not to cut them off immediately. In fact, you might want to whisper a quick prayer and ask the Holy Spirit to help you discern what's happening. Sometimes people need to share a painful experience or a pressing problem, and they just can't wait until the right point in the agenda. If as the facilitator you feel that they should continue, then let them continue. If the person wants to talk about himself or herself every week, well, that's another problem.

Lastly, if you find that your group likes to spend the first part of the meeting catching up with each other. Don't fight it. In fact, you might change your prayer time to the start of the meeting and pray right after everyone has caught up.

Then, you can start your study. Remember you are leading a group, not just leading a meeting.

Choosing Your Group's Next Study

Selecting the right study for your group is important, but how you select the study may be more important. Adult learners learn best in the area of their felt needs. The best study in the world won't work with an uninterested group. To guarantee that a study is the right fit for your group, here are a few things to consider:

1.   How long has your group been together?

If your group has just start or is less than six months old, chances are that your group members won't have much of an opinion about what to study next. In fact, taking too much time to decide on the next study might cause your group to falter.

Over the years, I've heard the conversation go like this when the leader presents three or four possible studies:

Leader: "Which study looks good to you guys?"

Group: "They all look good. Why don't you pick one?"

It happens every time. If you send the group to the Christian bookstore or to the internet, well, forget it. There are so many choices. They will never decide.

As the leader, go ahead and choose the next study before the current study ends. Introduce the study to the group and ask them if they would like to study it next. More than likely, the group will agree and you can move forward with confidence.

If your group is more than six months old, forget everything that I just said. If your group doesn't have buy-in for the next study, they might be bored, they might be frustrated, or they might leave. Again, midway through the current study, ask the group what they would be interested in studying next. But, this time, don't bring a study along with you. If established group members feel ownership in the group, they will want to have a voice. If they don't feel ownership, then what in the world are you doing?

Ask the group to share topics of interest or even specific studies they are interested in doing. Have group members research the studies on the internet, view video content online, or even print out the first lesson for the group to sample. Then, together as a group decide which study to do next.

2.   Who's in your group? New believers, maturing believers, or Bible connoisseurs?

Newer believers will need more direction. More mature believers will need less direction, if any. Take the situational leadership model on this. The less knowledgeable the group, then the more input they will need from the leader. The more knowledgeable the group, then they will only need someone to facilitate the decision-making. But, don't be mistaken— even experienced group members can drop the ball. As the leader, you must follow through in helping the group reach a decision. It won't decide itself.

Then, there's a third category – Bible connoisseurs. These are the folks who have consumed material from the best of the best. Any general, poorly produced, old-school Bible study will not do. They only want to learn from the pros. Their idea of going deeper is listening to the teacher who will tantalize them with a morsel of Bible trivia that they've never come across. Bible connoisseurs are in need of a service project, not "deeper" teaching.

3.   Should you go with consensus or the majority?

If you want to keep your group together, go with consensus. If you would like to quickly form a new group, then go with the majority. If 60 percent want one study, but 40 percent want another and you go with the 60 percent, you have effectively split the group. If everyone agrees together on a study, then they will stay. But, what if they can't agree?

If it's a 60/40 decision, then you should do one study now and plan to do the other study next. There's no reason to divide your group over choosing a study. Now, if you have one group member who likes to dictate to everyone else, that's an entirely different problem.

4.   If the study doesn't connect, punt.

Sooner or later every group gets into a study that they just don't like. Rather than persevere through a study that doesn't connect, recycle it. I mean in the trash. Find another study. Nowhere in the Bible does it command, "Thou shalt complete every lousy study thy group commences." Find something else.

"But, we spent 12 bucks a pop on the study guides." Ebay, my friend, ebay.

Years ago, when I knew less about small groups, one group leader nearly faced mutiny. The group had not talked about plans for the summer. But, most of the group had assumed that they would take a break and do some fun things together. On the night of their last lesson in their study, the group leader showed up with a fresh set of brand new study guides under his arm. He wanted the group to get closer to Jesus that summer. From what I heard, the leader came close to meeting Jesus in heaven that night.

Needless to say, there was no group meeting that summer. There almost wasn't a group, except that they really liked each other. The group continued on with another leader eventually.

By following these steps, your group can certainly get closer deciding on a study that will meet their needs and keep their interest. By avoiding some pitfalls as you facilitate the decision-making process, you can keep the group intact and keep your head, I mean role, as leader.

Dealing with Gossip and Conflict in Your Group

A couple of guys in our small group in California would wander out to the sidewalk after the meeting each week to smoke. They would just hang around in front of our house and talk. The other guys in the group were a little jealous of their fellowship and considered taking up the habit themselves.

Someone from another group heard about our smokers. Then, that person passed the news to a member of her group. The third person in the chain approached me at church one day, "I heard that you've got group members who smoke in front of your house every week. That must be embarrassing for a pastor."

I replied, "Yes, it's terrible. I wish they wouldn't smoke. But, I've heard that some groups are full of gossips."

Gossip is a small group killer. There is nothing more fatal to a small group than gossip. It is the deadliest sin in group life.

The Bible teaches that "a gossip separates close friends" (Proverbs 16:28) and "a gossip betrays a confidence; so avoid anyone who talks too much" (Proverbs 20:19). The Apostle Paul includes gossip on the sin lists in Romans 1 and 2 Corinthians 12 along with murder, envy, strife, jealousy, rage and deceit. Gossip is serious business. So, what do you do when it shows up in your group?

Be Proactive. Even though your group is filled with wonderful people, the first place to deal with gossip is on the first day of the group. As your group talks about their group values, you should formulate a group agreement. These are simply the things the entire group agrees to (see page 40). A key value for your group is confidentiality. What is said in the group needs to stay in the group. Period. Nothing in the group – comment, prayer request, joke, or off-the-cuff remark – should be repeated outside of the group.

Sometimes the rules get blurry. Let's say a group member requests prayer for a mutual friend, who is not in the group. Let's call her Jane. Jane is having some tests for a serious health problem. One day you bump into Jane's husband and tell him that you are praying for Jane and her health issues. The problem is that Jane hasn't said anything to her husband. She was afraid that the news would affect his heart condition, so she didn't want to worry him unnecessarily. (This is a fictitious story. I am not telling tales out of school here). Now, you get the picture.

Gossip, as benign as it might seem, is a missile that will sink the whole ship. Who would ever share another prayer request or personal issue in front of someone they feel that they can't trust? If the group lacks trust, relationships are broken down. There is no more group.

Confidentiality is the foundation of group life. Creating a small group agreement and reviewing it periodically will help to insure trust in the group.

Gossip discussed in the group is equally dangerous. Gossip shuts down trust. Even if the gossip is about someone outside of the group, it certainly makes the group wonder what this person says about them behind their backs. Gossip of any kind will diminish trust in the group. If the group lacks trust, then the members will not open up. The leader should redirect the gossiping member with "Let's keep our discussion to those present in the group." Then, take the member aside and privately talk to them about gossiping and the harm it can bring to a group.

What is gossip? Well, the rule of thumb is that if the person you are talking to is not part of the problem or part of the solution, then it's gossip.

Act Quickly. If something about your group is told outside of the group, deal with it as soon as you are aware of the incident. Don't interview every member of the group. The offended person should go directly to the offender. As Ross Perot once said, "If you see a snake, kill it. Don't appoint a committee on snakes." As Jesus said, "If your brother or sister sins, go and point out their fault, just between the two of you" (Matthew 18:15). If the offended person isn't willing, then you as the group leader must step in.

The first step is to pray and ask God for wisdom. Ask Him to prepare the way and to work on the offender in advance. If you're eager to confront the offender, then you should probably pray some more. If you're reluctant to confront, then you're probably in the right place.

Unless you heard the offender tell the gossip yourself, you must give them the benefit of the doubt. Tell them what was said outside of the group, and let them know the harm that it caused. Hopefully, they will admit their fault before you have to ask them directly. If they don't own it, then you have to ask: "Do you know who told this outside of the group?"

If they admit to the gossip, then they should be given an opportunity to confess to the group. If they don't admit it, then you must take the next step and bring a person with you who either heard the gossip or is somehow involved in the incident (Matthew 18:16).

If the person did gossip, but won't admit to it, more than likely, he will stop coming to the group on his own. Most people are not so callus as to offend the group, lie about it, and then continue participating in the group. But, don't be surprised.

Bring the issue up during a group meeting. If the person is repentant, then give him an opportunity to confess to the group and seek the group's forgiveness. The best scenario is that the group will forgive and everyone will be reconciled. This is ideal. But, it may take time for the group to trust the person again. Reconciliation isn't necessarily automatic with forgiveness. Over time, as the group bears with one another, they will be able to trust each other again.

If the person won't admit their fault, then the gossip must be addressed in the group in the person's presence. This shouldn't be presented in an accusatory way, but simply stated: "Someone in the group broke the group's confidentiality by saying something private outside of the group. What do you know about this? How did this affect the group?" The offender might come to repentance in the meeting.

As a last resort, if the group is certain about who committed the offense, then the group needs to ask the offender to leave the group. Jesus taught us, "If they still refuse to listen, tell it to the church; and if they refuse to listen even to the church, treat them as you would a pagan or a tax collector" (Matthew 18:17). In this case the "church" is the group.

The question is how should believers treat "pagans and tax collectors?" As with anyone who is not in relationship with God, believers should love them, even if they're an enemy (Matthew 5:44) and challenge them with the need for repentance. When the person repents, then the process of reconciliation should begin.

Few other issues are as harmful as gossip in a small group. But, if the leader deals with the issue quickly, chances are the group will remain strong. If the issue is not dealt with, it won't go away. In fact, it will become a greater problem.

Gossip is not just a bad habit, it is a prideful sin. The gossip is pleased to divulge information that other people don't have. It makes them feel powerful. As a group leader, the issue becomes how to serve a person who needs gossip to make them feel significant. What are they lacking? What are they misunderstanding about their relationship with Christ?

Managing the Tension between Discussing the Lesson and Personal Sharing

Striking a balance between relationships and Bible study can be challenging in a group meeting. Often leaders fear their groups will go to one of two extremes during their meetings. Either the group would be a bunch of Bible eggheads who care for God's Word but don't really care much for each other, or the group meeting would become a freewheeling discussion that is no more than a pooling of ignorance. There is a balance, but it's not the same for every group.

You need to ask, "Why did your group get together in the first place?" People join small groups for various reasons. They want to get to know other believers. They want a better understanding of God's Word. They want to feel that they belong. They need acceptance. They want encouragement and accountability. The pastor told them it was a good idea. There are many reasons.

While most group meetings involve a Bible study, the group is not a class gathered to learn lessons. There are other settings for that. It's always a good idea to talk to the group about their expectations. How many studies would the group like to do in the course of a year? How many meetings out of the month should focus on a study? How many meetings should focus on group life, serving, worship, outreach, or something else? The group may be on the same page, but you don't know until you've had the conversation and decided things together.

The personalities of your group members will also impact the dynamic in your meetings. Are your group members task-oriented or relationship-oriented? What are you? When you lead the discussion are you attempting to cover all of the questions or are you interested in what everyone has to say? If you tend to be more task-oriented, then your goal is to complete the lesson. If you're more relationship-oriented, then you might be tempted to throw the book out of the window and just let everybody talk.

Rather than resorting to an extreme, reach in the opposite direction. Task-oriented folks should train themselves to encourage personal sharing in the group. Maybe even have a night where folks share their spiritual journey and dispense with the lesson all together. When relationship-oriented folks lead a lesson, they should make sure good progress is made in the lesson, otherwise, they might frustrate some of the group members.

Selecting the right curriculum to facilitate discussion is also important. Some small group studies have as many as 30 questions. This is far too much to attempt to cover in a 45-60 minute group discussion. (The entire meeting from welcoming group members as they arrive until after the refreshments at the end is typically 90–120 minutes). The group leader should prioritize the questions according to their significance to the group and to the discussion. If the group has 10-12 people who actively participate, you might not need more than five or six good questions for the entire discussion. You should also consider sub-grouping during the discussion, so everyone can get their word in. The goal is to engage your group members, not just to complete a lesson.

Be aware of your group environment. Often God does his best work in the unplanned moments of group life. The leader needs to take cues from the group members as well as the Holy Spirit to determine when to pause the curriculum and allow a group member to share.

If a group member becomes a little teary, it's good to pause and take notice: "Dave, I see that things are a little tender right now. Would you like to talk about it?" He may or may not want to unpack what he's dealing with right then, but he will appreciate your sensitivity. To just continue the lesson without acknowledging what's going on is essentially telling Dave, "I'm not sure what your problem is, but we've got a lesson to finish."

I was leading a group discussion a few years ago. We were several questions into the study when one of the group members began telling a story. Her story had nothing to do with the question that I had just asked. It had nothing to do with the lesson. We all gave her our attention and listened carefully.

I quietly prayed and asked God for direction, "Lord, should I let her continue or do we need to move on?" The rest of the group seemed to be attentive to her story. I didn't feel any gut check about redirecting the discussion. She finished. The group responded. Then, we continued with the discussion.

Later, while the group was sharing dessert, the lady's husband pulled me aside. He said, "I can't believe she told that story tonight. She hasn't talked about that for 30 years." Even though her story was off-topic, after 30 years, she was ready to share. The time was right for her. The rest of the group made the timing right for us as well. Can you imagine the damage that might have been done if we had moved on?

Building relationships and doing Bible study is a balance in any small group. If you're going to err one way or the other, then err toward building relationships. Don't dispense with Bible study, but remember that small groups are life on life. It's not life on curriculum.

Knowing When to Refer Members for Appropriate Care

Group life is messy. People will come to your group looking neat and clean. They are well mannered. Then, they start opening up. Group is a safe place to share the stuff that they're wrestling with, and then the problems come out. Rather than throwing your hands up in the air, congratulation yourself. Your group is actually working. If no one in your group has a problem, then your group has a problem.

The question, then, is not if a group member has a problem. The question is what to do once problems are identified. There will always be problems.

What kind of need does the person have? Are you dealing with a past hurt, an abusive situation, an addiction, a job loss, a financial problem, sinful behavior, or something else? The type of need will largely determine what your group can and should do.

For example, if the person has a large financial need, then before your group starts helping financially, you should check with church staff and have them assess the need. Staff members who serve with benevolence have pretty good discernment to know who has a legitimate need and who's trying to scam the group. Unfortunately, some groups have been taken for a ride. There are also many resources in the community that could be of help. Your group can still help, but the help should be offered in coordination with the church staff.

What help seems to be working? As your group gives their attention to a hurting group member and listens, how is that helping them? Do they feel better after they talk things out or does this add fuel to the fire? When your group prays for the member's needs, what is the result? Does your group member find peace? Many people just need to know that other people care, that they are accepted as they are, and that it's normal for them to be experiencing this. If prayer and group support is encouraging to them, then keep it up.

A word of caution: Your group should avoid "fixing." Let group members talk without giving each other advice. Give them the gift of your attention without interrupting, telling your own story, or trying to solve their problem. They need to be validated by being heard. Sometimes a listening ear is all they need.

How is the care of the hurting person affecting the group? Most small groups are designed primarily as Bible study groups. Your group can offer care and support, but should be centered on a Bible study. If the hurting person in your group wants to turn your Bible study group into their personal support group, this can certainly cause some tension. Check-in with your other group members. Are they willing to serve or are they becoming weary in well-doing? Can the hurting person participate in group life, share what they need to share, but not make the group about them? You don't want to forfeit the rest of your group members over one member who dominates the group with their problems.

How is the Holy Spirit directing you? When you pray for this person, what are you prompted to do? If the Spirit prompts you to buy groceries, then go buy groceries.

What's your motive? Do you want to help because helping makes you feel good? Do you need to be needed? It's good to check-in with wise counsel. One member of my group was helping a friend with some bills. When I asked, "What do you feel led to do?"

He said, "I'm co-dependent. I feel led to fix the whole thing." That was one of the most honest moments in our group.

The Bible tells us to "bear one another's burdens" (Galatians 6:2), but it also tells us that "each one should carry their own load" (Galatians 6:5). When something becomes too heavy for another, the group should pitch in and help, but the group must avoid doing things for other people what they should be doing for themselves. This creates an unhealthy dependency that won't do anybody any good.

Check-in with your coach. If you feel out of your depth on something, it's not necessarily time to pass the problem along. God may be using the situation to stretch you and to show you how he intends to use you. Your coach is a great resource to determine how you should be involved.

What other resources are available? If a group member is dealing with an issue, a support group that addresses that particular issue would be a great resource for them. You can find groups in your church or community for Divorce, Separation, Grief, Substance Abuse, Single Parents, Single Mothers, Blended Families, Grandparents Raising Grandchildren, Marriage Issues, Financial Issues, and others. Sometimes it's helpful for a person dealing with the loss of a loved one to attend a grief support group in addition to your group meeting. Ideally, their grief issues for the most part are addressed in the support group, and then they can participate in the small group Bible study as well. That doesn't mean that they will never bring up their grief, but they will more fully process their grief in a designated support group.

If after all of this, the hurting person just doesn't seem to be getting help, it's probably time to refer them to a pastor or a licensed counselor. Your coach or your pastor is probably aware of counselors in the area to recommend.

If the hurting member won't follow direction regarding what's appropriate in group, then it's time for a difficult conversation. The presence of a narcissistic person will destroy your group. If after several personal conversations with them, they continue to dominate the group with their issues, you must stop this. Clearly redirect them in group: "Now, we have talked about this. This is not something that we are going to discuss here." Sometimes a look and a shake of the head will do it. I pray that your group never gets to this point with anyone, but if it does, you have to consider the good of the entire group.

This is about the time when a leader will say, "I didn't sign up for this." No, you didn't, but God did.

How Far Should You Go in Accommodating Group Members?

People are busy. There is no doubt about it. Often job schedules, travel schedules, family schedules, and numerous other activities will dictate against the group meeting. When the current arrangement works for most of the group, the dilemma is how much to change for a few without losing everybody else in the process.

First, what is the issue? Maybe something significant has changed in a group member's schedule, and they are no longer able to make the group meeting on your designated meeting day. There are some things that people just can't control – a standing meeting at work is now occupying the group meeting time, a major project is demanding overtime, a family situation is conflicting with the group time – these are all legitimate issues. There are also things people can control that might conflict with the group – the member has decided to take a class on the group meeting day, his child's sports practice is at the same time as group, she's not a morning person and just can't get up that early – these are also legitimate issues, but they are preferences.

Is the schedule conflict temporary or permanent? Has their schedule become too crowded to even participate in the group? All of these factors will play into the group's decision.

Second, who raised the issue? People do what they choose to do. Even if a lot of things are being thrown at them, they will ultimately do what they want to do. So, the question here is — who is proposing the change?

If the member wants to continue with the group, then the member will ask the group to consider a change. "Guys, I really hate to inconvenience you, but I can't meet on Tuesday's for lunch because my boss moved a mandatory weekly meeting to that day and time. Would you consider meeting on another day, so I can participate in the group?" That's a reasonable request that the group should consider.

If another group member is intervening on the member's behalf, you must determine if this is what the member in question really wants. Your group could possibly move heaven and earth to accommodate the member, when the member actually was content to just skip the meeting for a while. You certainly don't want the whole group to change their schedules only to find that the one they changed for can't make it anyway. This happens more often than you might imagine.

Next, what defines the group anyway? Is the group just the members who show up for the meetings? Is it the group roster? What is the group? Think about it this way: if a member of your family couldn't eat dinner with the rest of the family, are they no longer a family member? But, if the same family member is estranged from the family, what do we do then?

If the group is the meeting, then commitment is determined by tardiness and absences. But, isn't a group more than a meeting? A group is more like a family. There is a commitment to each other, even if there is an issue with the commitment to the meeting.

Every group goes through challenging seasons. And, there are even times when scheduling conflicts can't be resolved, so a group member has to move on. A group is a living thing. It is constantly changing. New members are added, and sometimes even long-time members move along. This is a normal part of group life. Don't panic.

But, if your group is more than just a meeting, then continue to invite your group members who can't regularly attend the meeting to be involved in other aspects of group life. Include them in group service projects, parties, and other activities. Keep them on your email list, unless they intentionally choose to join another group. If the member is dealing with a ridiculously busy schedule, even a text message from other members is significant.

What is the group willing to do? The entire group should consider the situation and the options together. Is the situation beyond the group member's control? Did the group member prioritize something else over the group meeting? What options does the group have? The entire group should decide together whether they need to make a change to accommodate a member's schedule. Don't put yourself in a leader versus group member decision, and certainly don't dictate to your group. You are the group leader, not the group owner.

In my group, one member decided that he didn't want to pay around $10 for lunch any more. He was more of a dollar menu kind of guy. He was also a member of another small group in addition to ours. The group decided to wish him well, but didn't move to Wendy's or Taco Bell.

Another group member kept getting called into meetings in another city on Thursdays, but Wednesday were typically good for him. So, the group chose to move to Wednesdays so he could participate.

Our group met in restaurants up and down a busy road where we live in South Carolina. We never ran out of restaurants even though we changed every month. The group decided together where to meet each month. For one season, the group had ventured a little too far down the road for some of the guys to get to back to work on time, so the group chose restaurants closer to their businesses.

Whether your group chooses to change days or locations, the key is for the whole group to make the decision together. It's a decision that needs to work for everyone.

What is the result of the change? If your group decided move the meeting to accommodate the group member, did it work out? Is he still involved in the group? If so, then your group can continue as normal.

If after trying to accommodate the group member, and he doesn't come after several weeks to months, then it's time for a conversation with the member. This shouldn't be a guilt-induced, brow beating. But, obviously something else is going on with this group member. What's going on with him personally? Did something happen in the group? Did something happen outside of the group?

If the group member hasn't rejoined the group after the change, then you should be reluctant to make another change for this group member. Sometimes the people you go the greatest lengths to reach still never show up. I learned this when I reorganized an entire Bible college class schedule for a student who needed to complete the class and needed to participate on a mission trip in order to graduate. After his mission trip, the class reconvened only to discover that the student we tried to accommodate never returned.

Every group leader wants to be the good shepherd who will leave the 99 and go after the one. If you go to extremes, however, you might alienate the rest of the group and find yourself in a small group of two.

You can't keep every group member for life. That's just not possible. After the group has done everything they can, if the group member can't participate, then it might be time to move on.

How to Meet Members' Emotional Needs

Small groups can meet some of every members' basic emotional needs. Everyone needs to feel that they belong. This is a high value among groups. The Bible teaches, "Just as each of us has one body with many members, and these members do not all have the same function, so in Christ we who are many form one body, and each member belongs to all the others" (Romans 12:4-5). Everyone wants to be included by others. Your group is the place where members and visitors are always included. You belong.

Everyone also needs to feel accepted. Regardless of where they've come from or what they've done, your group is a place where people can come as they are to learn, to connect and to encourage each other. That doesn't mean that your group will allow anyone to stay where they are. If there are things going on in their lives that are harmful or damaging to their well-being and spiritual growth, then it's the group's place to address these things in their lives. Sometimes people are blind to things about themselves that are very obvious to others. The group should never approach anyone with a judgmental or self-righteous attitude. The rest of the group has their issues too.

You have to accept people where they are. Think about it. Where else are you going to accept them? I suppose you could put some prerequisites for being accepted into your group. But, why make it harder to be accepted in your group than it is to be accepted by Jesus himself?

While groups can meet some important emotional needs for your members, groups can't meet all of their emotional needs. And, they shouldn't try to meet all of their emotional needs either. While the Bible does tell believers to bear one another's burdens (Galatians 6:2), it also teaches that each one should carry his own load (Galatians 6:5). John Townsend and Henry Cloud do a great job of explaining this in their book, Boundaries.

As a group, you can help people process what's going on in their lives. You can care for them. You can pray for them. You can follow up with them. But, you can't allow the needs of one member to dominate the group. If you begin to see this happen, you need to gently recommend other resources to address their issues. At that point a support group or a counselor could help them work through their issues. If members are struggling in a relationship or with a life controlling problem, the group can certainly support them in their progress, but the group cannot become their "support group."

Never kick them out of your group. In fact, the leader should let them know that they are welcome to continue in the group for Bible study and that the group will gladly support them in their journey. But, the work that needs to be done has to happen in another setting.

It's important to know what you can and cannot do in a group. You can offer teaching from God's Word. You can offer friendship. You can offer prayer. You can offer acceptance and belonging. You can't offer anything that caters solely to one group member and excludes the others. You can't take on all their problems. You can't meet all of their emotional needs. You can't do for them what only God can. But, you can keep pointing them back to God.

What is your group carrying for your members? Where might your group be trying to carry the member's whole load as well? How do you know when it's time to ask for help? Check in with your coach and determine what help is truly helpful.

Group Members and Homework

Group members, like everybody else, are busy people. "But, if they're really committed, they would do their homework," you might object. What if they're really committed and show up to the group most weeks? The question of homework raises several issues about expectations and gifts in your group.

What is your goal concerning homework? What is the purpose of homework? If the center of the group is sharing life together, then the preparation comes from your life experiences. If the group is centered on a lesson, then by doing homework, each group member is prepared for the discussion. Statistically, half of the group members will do homework and the other half won't. As the group leader, it's important to include everybody in the discussion. Group members who are prepared will be quick with their answers.

Group members who didn't prepare will need a little more time to respond.

What expectations have been set by the group? Has the group agreed to homework? Did the group choose the study together and go into it with eyes wide open? Did they understand how much homework would be involved? Or did the group leader spring the study on them?

Group expectations are best decided together as a group. Everyone should agree on what the group will be discussing as well as any expectations for homework, rotating leadership, bringing refreshments, etc. If the group leader chooses to assign homework without the group's consent, then don't be surprised by a lack of participation.

What benefit is there to doing homework? If the group has prepared in advance, then you understand that the lesson will be easier to lead. But, what's in it for the group? Other than avoiding the group leader's wrath, what do they get out of it?

Group members who spend time studying the topic in God's Word will definitely benefit from spending time in God's Word. The principles will stick with them longer. These are all great things if the entire group agrees to it. Be clear about what is expected: self-study, daily reading, reviewing the discussion questions, or even attending the Sunday service together.

What if the group can't live up to the agreement? One summer my group decided to study a great Christian book. Our assignment was to read and discuss one chapter per week. We all agreed. Then, reality set in. While everyone attended the group each week, most of the members, including the leader, had trouble getting to the chapter every week. Yet, we were committed to completing the study.

Our solution was simple: at least one group member would read the assigned chapter each week, give the group a summary, and lead the discussion. This was great for many reasons. Our guilt was relieved. Everyone led at least twice that Summer, so they read at least two chapters. The group didn't fall apart. Then, of course, we agreed to never attempt another book study again.

Asking for homework might be revealing a teaching gift. Carl George has wisely said that if the group leader is assigning homework, then more than likely, the group leader has a teaching gift. Teachers make homework assignments. His suggestion is not to use the teaching gift to assign homework. Instead, the group leader should use his gift to do the homework themselves, and then teach the group along with the group discussion. While you don't want to turn the group into a class, the group leader's teaching gift can certainly enhance the discussion. Of course, the other alternative would be for the group leader to teach a Sunday School class or a Bible Institute type class rather than leading a group.

Expectations can run awry unless they are clear, reasonable and accountable. The key is buy-in from the group. Adult learners are motivated by what interests them. Imposing something on them is highly de-motivating. By taking the time to agree together as a group, you will greatly reduce frustration all of the way around.

How to Know When God is Speaking to You

"I believe that God is directing me to ..." How do you handle this statement in a group? Whether the group member feels led to quit his job, move to another state, or end a relationship, how do you help your group member discern the truth?

From the very beginning, God has been in relationship with people. Today, believers are not walking in the garden with God in the cool of the day or getting inspiration to write new books of the Bible, but God does speak to his people. The question is how do you know that it's actually God and not wishful thinking or indigestion? Here are some tests for what you might be hearing.

1.   What does the Bible say?

As followers of Christ hold that the Bible is God's Word. Any direction attributed to God must square up with God's Word. God isn't going to contradict himself. That wouldn't make any sense.

For instance, if your group member feels closest to God in nature, so he feels led to quit his job and spend more time seeking God out in the woods. The problem is that he's not independently wealthy and isn't ready to retire. His wife will have to carry the load of the family finances. She hasn't worked outside of the home for years, and he would basically expect her to do everything she's doing now, plus provide the total family income. This may seem farfetched, but in over 25 years of ministry, there have been some doozies. This one is hypothetical, however.

While it may seem spiritual to connect with God in a peaceful place, it's also spiritual to provide for the needs of your family. If you don't, you're worse than an infidel (1 Timothy 5:8, KJV). When God's leading conveniently confirms one's own desires and violates God's Word, then you must question whether the person has actually heard from God.

This is just a silly example, but some people have felt led to leave their spouse, stop paying their taxes, stop giving to the church, buy a new car, drill an oil well in a specific spot – you name it. While God does speak to believers, the primary way he speaks is through the Bible. If what they are hearing doesn't line up with Scripture, then they need to listen again.

2.   How does it line up with other circumstances?

Sometimes people feel a leading from God to escape a problem. Instead they should allow God to help them work through problems. They come out better people on the other side. "But, my wife just left me. It's the perfect time for me to go to the mission field." Not so fast there, buddy. On the Holms-Rahe Stress Test, divorce is one of the highest stressors there is. If you add leaving your home, friends, and your church to taking on a new job, a new culture, a new climate, a new language, and so on, not to mention the spiritual toll of divorce, it's the recipe for disaster.

But, sometimes the circumstances line up. When the person is not in the middle of a problem, when they feel a leading and finances line up, and the house sells, and the spouse agrees, God's plan just might be coming together.

3. Has the person sought godly counsel?

Who has the person consulted on this leading? Have they talked to mature believers and pastors who will ask the hard questions and tell them the truth? Or, have they just sought out people who would easily agree with them? Every believer needs people in their lives who love them, but aren't impressed with them.

They shouldn't be in a hurry for quick affirmation. It's important to ask others to discuss the potential leading and to pray with them. God often uses others to confirm or dispute a leading.

4. What do the other group members sense in their gut?

When the group first hears the news, what is their reaction? What do the faces around the room say? As you've spent time together, you've started to get to know each other, good or bad. Does this news fall in the category of group excitement or "Here we go again?"

5. What other confirmation have they received?

Is there independent confirmation? Someone out of the blue says, "You would be really good at..." then describes exactly what the person feels led to do without any knowledge of the leading. The Lord works in mysterious ways, but not in careless ways.

If the person is gaining confirmation from dreams or fortune cookies, then he needs a little help. If he feels led to buy a new white car, suddenly he will see white cars all around him. Guess what? They were already there.

6. What if they're unwilling to listen to others?

There is a place for godly counsel, and then there's a place for the person to make his own decision. Even if he makes a mistake, it's his decision. If you and the group strongly feel that he is in error, once you've had your say, don't continue to bash him. But, you also don't need to offer support for the endeavor. The Bible tells us, "Sometimes it takes a painful experience to make us change our ways." (Proverbs 20:30, GNT). If the member will not listen to the group, then there's no choice but to allow them to have the experience and learn from it. You should continue to pray for the person and show concern for him. You should also avoid trying to rescue the person when things go wrong.

If the person is particularly obnoxious about it, then the group might need to implement the disciplinary teaching in Matthew 18:15-17. See page 124 for the practical implementation of this teaching. The last resort would be for the group and the individual to part ways.

Sometimes people get caught up in the moment and feel that God is calling them. Sometimes God does. How do you know? If it's a calling, then it will last. If it's a temporary feeling, then it will pass – unless the person has already told people, then pride might get in the way.

You want to encourage people to listen to God. These situations come with a label – "Handle with Care." But, as you guide your members through these criteria to confirm their callings – God's Word, circumstances, godly counsel – God's leading will become clear. Anybody can make mistakes along the way. But, if you don't try to discern God's voice, then you never will. The goal is to hear God more clearly with less confusion. It's possible to lead your group members there.

If you have further questions, please send them to info@allenwhite.org. The author might blog about them or add them to a future edition of this book.

CHAPTER 8
STARTING NEW GROUPS

Ending Your Group

Small groups aren't meant for last forever. But, how do you end it? Do you gather your group members together for an uncomfortable conversation?

"It's not you. It's us. Can we just be friends?"

While some groups can last 20 years or more, most groups simply can't run that distance. That's okay. After all, we have friends for a reason, friends for a season, and friends for a lifetime. But, how do you know when your small group has run its course? If your group is no longer fulfilling its mission, then it's definitely time to move on.

Over time, groups tend to lose their edge. Group life demonstrates a tension between speaking the truth in love (Ephesians 4:15) and bearing one another's burdens (Galatians 6:2). The balance lies in correcting each other and understanding each other. When a group starts, a member's weaknesses and failures seem more obvious.

"Why does he do that?"

"Why does she treat them that way?"

But, over time, the group begins to understand why. Rather than saying, "You might have more success with a gentler approach," we find ourselves saying things like, "He's a little rough around the edges. His childhood was a nightmare. We understand." Since the group has accepted the behavior as part of the person's makeup, there is no expectation for change. And, if people don't change, then they don't grow.

Deep seated problems aren't resolved over night. They take a great deal of work and are often beyond the scope of the group's ministry (read in the section called "Knowing When to Refer Members for Appropriate Care on page 131). The problem comes when our understanding becomes enabling.

The goal of every group should be to help each other reflect Christ. When a group has been together for a while and loses its edge of truth, it no longer helps anyone fulfill the goal. Iron isn't sharpening iron. If your group started as a Gensu knife, but has dulled and become a butter knife, then it's time to regroup. If your group can regain its edge, that's great. If not, then it's time to disperse and form new groups.

Another time to think about ending your group is when the group has significantly lost members. Every group loses members. It's not a bad group. Life just gets in the way. A group member moves out of town. A new job or family activity conflicts with the group's meeting day. Sooner or later, good group members will leave for good reasons.

After four years leading my group, we only had two original members. One of them was me. While there were only two in the "senior class," we had a couple of juniors, a few sophomores, and a couple of freshmen. If Jamie and I had been the only two left in the group, we might have gotten together now and then, but we probably wouldn't meet every week for a Bible study. When your group gets down to just a couple of people, it's time to reconsider and rebuild – either by invitation or forming a new group. But, sometimes new members won't stick.

No one likes to see their good group members go. If you've become close friends, you certainly don't want things to come to an end. If your group is beginning to see the beginning of the end, act now to turn things around. Become a more welcoming and including group. Invite prospects to attend. Develop your new freshman classes. Otherwise, "us four" will eventually become "no more."

Every group goes through a lifecycle. There is an initial period when every one is new, then they start to get to know each other on a deeper level. As the group becomes better acquainted, they discover the truth to the title of John Ortberg's book, *Everybody's Normal Till You Get to Know Them*. The group has to adjust. Your members are real and have real problems. This is not the time to quit. Your members will go through difficult circumstances. This is not the time to quit. Someone in the group becomes particularly difficult. This is not the time to quit. Your group becomes stressful when it was supposed to be a sweet little Bible study. This is not the time to quit. Your group needs to stick together and work things out.

Difficult circumstances, even those difficulties produced by the group members, help everyone to grow. If you have a difficult group member, then you have an opportunity to learn to love a difficult person. If the needs of the group are overwhelming, then talk to your coach. Get additional help and resources. But, it's not time to quit.

Once the group has moved past the issue at hand and has settled somewhat, the time is right to consider ending your group. Once people have survived the dip in group life and seem to be on the upswing once again, this is the point your group might decide to change direction. Once your group has reached the 18-24 month point, then it's time to consider moving on.

Groups shouldn't stop in a hard place. They should consider ending the group in a successful place. There's a time to be pulled and stretched in different ways. There's a time to allow well-trained co-leaders who've shared the leadership of the group with you to branch out and begin their own group. There's a time for the "kids" in your group to reach out to others and have "grandkids." There's a time for you to take a break, then start another group with new members. Until everyone is reached or until Jesus comes back, there is work to do.

This is not easy. Groups, especially in North America, like to stay together. I've seen groups continue for 20 or 30 years. They are an extended family. They are close. Now, they're supposed to get a small group divorce? That's not what it's called, but it's definitely what breaking up feels like.

Forcing your group to end after a defined period of time is not the way to go. Considering the next step for the group is the way to go. For some groups, it's time to move on. They've lost their edge and aren't doing a lot of good anymore. Or, the group is full of leaders you developed. They need to lead – even if they lead the group and you leave. You could be their coach.

At 18-24 months, the group should consider their next steps. Maybe they'll move on. Maybe they'll continue. It's definitely worth the conversation.

The key to an effective transition is a group decision. You may have already decided to go, but the group must be prepared. Take the time to work through any outstanding issues with the group. When the time is right, then each member should pursue their next step.

Once the decision is made to discontinue the group, then it's time to celebrate. Have a party. Celebrate what the group has accomplished in its time together – people saved, spiritual growth, marriages saved, battles won, neighbors reached, new groups starting. Ending a group is not a defeat, so treat it like the victory it is. Ask your group member who's great at throwing parties to plan something big for the group. This is a significant milestone.

Leaving Your Group

I have left every group I have ever led, except for my family. I led a men's prayer breakfast that met at 6:00 in the morning, and I'm not a morning person. The group was made up of core members in the church. They were all solid citizens. Every one of them could lead a group, and many of them eventually did. After five years of leading this group, I had to evaluate my involvement in everything I was doing ministry-wise. I was even leading other groups. I determined that this group no longer needed me.

One morning, I announced to the group, "Guys, I am going to stop leading the group in two weeks. If you would like to continue meeting, you need to figure it out." And, I left. They appointed a new leader and continued on for many years. I slept in and poured myself into other things after a good night's sleep.

I left a home group I led. We had made a 12 month commitment. At the end of 12 months, the group opted not to continue. Members of that group eventually led groups themselves.

My wife and I left a couples' group we had led for several years. We moved out of town. The commute would have been difficult. We designated a new leader, who continued with the group.

In that same season, I led a small group team who met essentially as a small group, even though they were all leaders and coaches themselves. After meeting with them for a year, I quizzed them on how they would do the next small group launch if I wasn't there. Off the top of their heads, they knew exactly what to do. I had effectively worked myself out of a job. Six months later I left. My team led the small group ministry for the next year until my replacement was hired at the church. If I had stayed, I would have only been in the way.

I led a men's lunchtime group for four years. When I left the staff of the church this group was a part of, I continued to lead the group for a while, but I reached the conclusion that I was part of the group's past, not part of their future. I invited another member of the group to become the group leader. He had been part of the group for several years. He continued the group for four more years. Then, he passed the baton to a new leader a couple of years ago. That group is still going.

There are many reasons for the leader to leave the group. Sometimes it's a practical reason – the members of the group are ready to take on the leadership. Sometimes it's a logistical reason -- you're leaving town. Often the leader's absence gives an opportunity for someone else. When you're group is ready, it's time to leave.

Starting Your Next Group

If you are at this stage, you are in a great place. You have successfully transitioned your group to a new leader or successfully ended your group that was not going in the right direction. Either way, you've succeeded in building your new group.

Starting your new group is not much different that starting your original group. Check in with your coach or small group director. Make a list of names of people who might enjoy or benefit from the study. Pray over your list and start inviting.

If you are starting your next group in the same geographic area or at the same church, things can be a little tricky with your former group members. If you left your former group to a new leader, then you want to encourage your former group members to stay with the group and support the new leader. Otherwise, their group change will come across as undermining the new leader. Since you are inviting the new members of your group, if some of your former members are invited, but others aren't, this could lead to some significantly hard feelings. You simply want to avoid this. Start fresh. Don't allow this thought to deter you, but keep this in mind.

If your group ended because of the group dynamic – your group members weren't really growing spiritually or had lost their edge – you don't want to bring any element of that environment into your new group. For whatever reason, the makeup of your former group did not lend itself to spiritual growth. Some groups just don't gel for a variety of reasons previously discussed in this book. It's best to start fresh. Telling your previous group that they can't join your new group could be awkward. This would be a good occasion to involve your coach and ask him or her to explain these things to your group. You will need to be present in the discussion. The coach's words will come across as official notice that at your church new groups are formed with new members. If they would like to be a part of a new group, then maybe it's time to consider starting a group themselves.

Once you've crossed that hurdle, you become part of a wonderful new adventure. New members will find connection and acceptance. They will grow in significant ways. They will experience transformation through God's Word and the Holy Spirit's power. Your group will learn from Bible studies, life lessons, risks taken, and painful circumstances. They will reach out to the community serving many and inviting some to the group. You'll discover some have great potential to lead and need an opportunity to practice their gifts. One day, they may lead this group.

In the meantime, you might get the opportunity to coach your previous group and others. You will further develop yourself as a leader by pouring into the lives of other leaders.

Recommended Resources for Group Leaders

Leading Life-Changing Small Groups by Bill Donahue (Zondervan, 2012).

Leading Small Groups with Purpose by Steve Gladen (Baker Books, 2012).

Making Small Groups Work by Henry Cloud and John Townsend (Zondervan, 2003).

Nine Keys to Effective Small Group Leadership by Carl George (CDLM, 2007).

The Big Book of Small Groups by Jeffrey Arnold (IVP Connect, 2004).

World's Greatest Small Group by Michael Mack (Small Group Leadership, 2017).

ABOUT THE AUTHOR

Allen White has coached over 1,500 churches across North America as well as serving on staff at New Life Christian Center, California, and Brookwood Church, South Carolina. Allen teaches workshops for various churches and organizations, such as Saddleback Church and Willow Creek Canada, and is part of the Small Group Network (smallgroupnetwork.com), which has chapters in all fifty states and many country es. Allen offers courses, coaching groups, resources, and a weekly blog at allenwhite.org. He holds a BA in Biblical Studies and Missions and an MDiv in Christian Education from Evangel University, Springfield, Missouri.

Made in the USA
Middletown, DE
07 August 2020